BILLY CONNOLLY

Biography
RAMBLING AND LIFE ON THE ROAD

Juana Sarmiento Gaytan

TABLE OF CONTENTS

CHAPTER 1
GET YOUR KICKS . . .

WALKING is the typical mode of transportation for a Rambling Man, but there are occasions when he wants to travel from point A to point B quickly, and a bicycle or motorbike will suffice. It's simply having the ability to travel somewhere else quickly if you're unhappy where you are; a basic technique of keeping sane. And when you can adjust the picture smartly on two wheels, you usually have more fun doing it. When I was a kid, I got my first bicycle for Christmas. It was a purple New Hudson racing bike that provided me with the independence I craved. I could flee my home and ride through the countryside like a true Rambling Man. I had no food, no company, and nothing but water in a flask, yet I loved it. It felt fantastic just to be alone where no one could touch me or affect what I was doing. I had the impression that I could do or be whatever I desired. It was all up to me, which was a wonderful feeling. I'd go up to Loch Lomond or Helensburgh - small beach towns that were a world away from where I lived in the heart of Glasgow. I appreciated the fresh country air and wonderful light in the area around Loch Lomond. Made me come over all Sir Walter Scottish: breathes the guy, with spirit so dead, who never said to himself, This is my own, my original land!
Mountains, forests, lochs... maybe tourism will take off there one day, eh?
I was a Cub Scout in the 141 pack the first time I went up to Loch Lomond. Auchengillan was the largest camp I attended. The scouts sang around a totem pole, "We're riding on the crest of a wave, and the sun is shining."
Keep an eye out for passers-by as we keep our gaze fixed on the distant horizon. Those Scout camps instilled in me a love of the outdoors that has never faded, and after that first taste, I frequently returned to Loch Lomond on my bike. I'd sit by the lake to relax and make tea out of small twigs. There was always a strong aroma of tea and wood burning in the room. You may stop at any moment for a 'drum-up,' utilising community tobacco and sugar concealed in the stone walls by other bikers. I used to take off and go camping whenever I could when I was in my early teens. It always gave me a thrill to wake up and travel somewhere, to get on the road and end up

somewhere I'd never been before. It was an adventure, a getaway. I never gave much thought to any potential danger, and my father never asked where I was going - I just went. I'd wind up thousands of miles from home, sleeping beneath a cheap tent - often in the pouring rain - with no groundsheet and very little money for food. It never occurred to me that some people would think that was odd.

But cycling was more than just a way to get somewhere. I also like racing other boys on my bike. A couple of roundabouts were about two or three miles apart on the outside of the housing estate where I lived, leading off the Great Western Road. It was our own little racing circuit for myself and the other boys, going like the clappers down the road, then racing around the roundabouts three times and back to the finish line. It was difficult, especially in the cold. My cycling outfit back then consisted of long pants, a pullover, a thin windbreaker, fingerless gloves, and a pair of Reg Harris Fallowfield cycle shoes with Union Jacks on the tongues.

Cycling was simpler back then. Thirty years later, I couldn't imagine riding in public without my Vitus Duralinox machine and multi-colored spandex shorts. I wore green snakeskin spandex when I ran the London to Brighton charity race in the late 1980s. 'Big Yin, eh!' One of my opponents began picking on my tits. 'Those appear to be knickers!' 'Don't worry, mate,' I assured him. 'You'll just get to view the arse.'

Cyclists are usually nice individuals - while they're riding their bikes, that is. When they get off, they rejoin the rest of humanity. I was drawn to the friendship among riders as a child. I quickly realised that we needed each other. Things could go wrong, such as punctures, brake failure, or gear failure, so you had to rely on one another to keep going. If another person had a flat tire, you hopped off your bike and helped him, even if you were racing each other. The reasoning was that it made no sense for you to charge ahead. There was no satisfaction in proclaiming, 'I beat you by an hour,' when all he was doing was trying to mend his puncture. You had to collaborate.

Even though they are generally loners by nature, certain Rambling Men have a similar lore. They never feel lonely on the road and do not desire company, but they do meet and converse with other people when they feel like it - sometimes to find a place to stay or to make some money - and they help one other out. Leon Ray Livingston, commonly known as 'A-No.1' or 'The Rambler', was a well-known 'hobo' in America. He was self-educated, and he wrote books about how to travel the 'hobo' manner and the 'hobo code'. During the Great Depression in America, when 'hobos' were in abundance, they devised a 'code' system for leaving critical messages for other travellers. These were usually secret symbols chalked, carved, or etched on signs and walls, indicating where to find clean drinking water, pointing to helpful people, or warning of danger or hostility in one form or another - such as unfriendly cops or aggressive animals. Hobos had their own names for items as well; if you ask for a 'banjo,' he'll offer you a frying pan. A 'barnacle' is someone who stays at the same work for a year, while a 'California newspaper' is a blanket. It's a highly developed little society that's kept hidden for good cause. A 'Hobo Convention' is currently taking place in Britt, Iowa, USA. Every year, a Hobo King and Queen are crowned, and the council members hold their annual meeting to discuss communal issues.

My little bike group was significantly less well-organised. We didn't leave any symbols, but we did give each other advice on how to keep your bike rust-free or where to get a good bicycle pump. Bicycle gear has become significantly more sophisticated over the years. Bicycle seats, for example, evolved into spongy pads. Some companies produced an oily, rubbery substance that they trapped between two layers of leather to create shaky seat covers. It felt sensual, which, as you can surely understand, had the potential to cause some new problems. I was ready to install one of those seat covers on my bike when I noticed a warning regarding 'penile numbness' in the handbook. The manufacturers recommended a method of treatment known as 'discreet massage'. 'Oh, yes?' 'Is that what they're calling it now?' I wondered. I began to wonder what would happen if the entire Tour de France team suffered from penile numbness and had to rely on 'discreet massage' during the ride. They'd never make it across the Pyrenees. They'd be exhausted from cycling into fields and becoming blind!

When I was in my twenties, I graduated to motorbikes and motor trikes. The main attraction was that I could travel further. I might ride to England, to Blackpool, or to the Isle of Skye in Scotland. It felt fantastic to escape on my motorcycle. I could travel far away to places where things were really different; places where people lived and spoke differently. I encountered several more Rambling Men on their motorcycles doing the same thing. They slept under the stars, sat around campfires, and played harmonicas and guitars, just like me. They didn't find it strange at all. I didn't either. There were groups of us all over, and it quickly became a movement. Journalists began to see an increasing number of people living their lives in this manner, and they began writing about it as a phenomenon. I read magazine articles about particular people from that movement and respected them, but no one knew what it was all about. We were just having fun and living in the present.

The sensation of riding a motorcycle is unparalleled. That cannot be obtained by driving a car. The wind does more than merely blow your hair. Strange fact: it causes the hippy beads around your neck to fly straight out horizontally ahead as you ride. Before I became a 'hippy' biker, I thought dressing like Marlon Brando in The Wild One made me more desirable to women. At the very least, it took the sting out of my acne. Brando, on the other hand, was an emblem of American gang culture, not a Rambling Man. We linked to the misunderstood, the lonely, the outsider in James Dean, who was not a Rambling Man either.

Although any roadworthy motorcycle will probably get you where you need to go, there's no denying the visual impact of riding a good machine. I started out with rather basic used motorcycles that required a lot of maintenance, but later on I had some beauties, such as my purple Harley-Davidson three-wheeler. That was one mean tricycle. I rode it in the 'bad boy' posture, reclining. It's a true 'Go screw yourself' attitude. People in beige sedans look quite old-fashioned. 'Don't stare at him, Dorothy; you'll be pregnant before you know it. He most likely has tattoos on his willy.'

I previously had a fantastic biker jacket created for a New Zealand tour. I was filming a TV episode in which I rode both the North and South Islands. It's a terrific place to ride a motorcycle. The tour's name, 'Too Old to Die Young,' was written on the back in Hells Angels-style lettering and with a skull emblem. It was fantastic. It was made for me by a woman in Los Angeles. She explained that she needed authorization from the Hells Angels crew because they are quite fussy about their appearance and trademarks. Anyway, I was out riding alone one morning in Wellington wearing my jacket when I saw I was being surrounded by teamsters from the Mongrel Mob, New Zealand's largest biker gang with a bad reputation. They surrounded me at a traffic light and dragged me down a side street. Because I was absolutely alone, I felt vulnerable. 'Where'd you buy your jacket?' one of them said. 'I acquired it in Los Angeles,' I explained. It was made by a young lady for me. She obtained permission.' 'Did she get permission?' They were quite assertive. I replied, 'Yeah, from the Hells Angels.' They went away and had a small conference, 'Urrrrrgggggurgggg.' Then they returned and replied, 'That's fine.' They backed down and allowed me to continue on my way. My TV team was furious because they didn't get any of that on film. And I didn't mention it onstage because I wanted to leave town in one piece.

On the way to Wellington, I saw a sign outside a bar that proclaimed, 'This Place Welcomes Bikers.' What does that have to do with a bar? I'm not going in, it says. I like bikers, but there's a type of biker I don't want to know who goes to a motorcycle bar. Fights are common, and they have effective weapons such as chains and padlocks. A padlock with a hanky wound to the handle is an excellent biker tool. The padlock is placed in your back pocket, and the hanky is hung. Prepared for action. A knock on the head with that object could be worse than a 'Glasgow kiss,' which is a sudden headbutt. Glasgow has a unique headbutt that must be experienced to be believed. You never want to be on the receiving end of that, and here's a trick to determine if a guy is ready to headbutt you: look at how his feet move. He'll put one foot in front of the other, like a boxer, to improve his balance. And he'll approach you with his head tilted to one side, then straighten up. Glasgow has a violent history and culture. Stephen Mulrine, a Glasgow poet, created a smashing poem called 'The Coming of the Wee Malkies' that is popular among children despite the fact that the verb 'to Malkie' refers to slashing someone with a razor. 'The Wee Malkies will get you,' people say, referring to a threat directed at children. That much sums up Glasgow. I'm all for 'hard man bravado' at four years old. When Glaswegians see someone with a bandage on his head, they will comment, 'Looks like he was talking when he should have been listening.' And if someone has a knife slash on his face, it's considered a "second prize." On one of my many visits to a hospital emergency department, I discovered that the international medical field's standard test for measuring a patient's level of consciousness after a brain injury was developed in Glasgow hospitals due to the high prevalence of injuries in the city following Saturday-night fights. It's known as the Glasgow Trauma Scale.

Newcastle, Australia, is a popular motorcycle destination. Backstage at the venue where I performed, a fantastic group of bikers worked. They had intricate tattooing on their bodies and braids in their hair. Their responsibilities included moving all of the scenery on and offstage. We clicked like a house on fire. They were enamoured by my Harley trike, which had appeared on the cover of a magazine. Backstage, they all started laughing when I mentioned the recent Newcastle earthquake during my concert. 'You'll notice I do my entire act with my feet pointing that direction,' I said to the crowd. I'm fucking off after one rumble! You can keep the roof up while I go over there.' The motorcycle gang told me after the event that during the earthquake, one of their friends, a large, bearded biker covered in tattoos, was being operated on in the hospital. They were all waiting in the waiting room for news. When the first major rumble came, they shouted, 'Everybody out!' and pushed all the mattresses onto the shore. So their friend was in a hospital bed on the beach. When he awoke, he was surrounded by palm trees and cockatoos, and he said, 'Oh! It's exactly like Earth!'

America is another fantastic place to ride a motorcycle. The states are linked by lengthy highways that are susceptible to weather damage, thus they are normally properly maintained. When I finally got to cycle the entire length of Route 66, I discovered that the road surfaces were astonishingly good. Route 66 is the world's most renowned road. How many other routes are sung about? Piccadilly, Bourbon Street, and Broadway are possibilities. The Champs-Elysées is mentioned in a few songs, but Route 66 is one of those fabled locations that many people want to see. Rambling Men are naturally drawn to it since it has come to signify the sense of escape, freedom, and adventure. When I was a young child fascinated by rock 'n' roll, I heard the phrase 'Get your kicks on Route 66' and pondered what on earth it meant. I informed my sister that I was sure it was pure magic. Thirty years later, I rode my tricycle for over 2,000 miles along it, from Chicago to Los Angeles, while filming a TV show about it.

I'd been to Chicago several times before, but I'd never seen it from the river. Before beginning my journey down Route 66, I glanced over the city from a boat on the Chicago River, from which I had a panoramic view of some of the tallest buildings in the United States. I attempted to visualise what it was like before the big fire of 1871, when it was a city of wooden structures. According to all accounts, it was a low-rise frontier hamlet serving as a gateway to the West. However, the fire destroyed practically everything in the city. Only one water tower survives, which I saw from my tricycle; it's virtually concealed among the skyscrapers. Following the fire, construction of steel and concrete castles commenced.

The Tribune Tower, a Gothic Revival structure with stripes reaching three-quarters of the way up and insane, castle-like turrets at the top, was one skyscraper that truly jumped out for me. Colonel Robert R. McCormick owned and published the Chicago Tribune. He'd been to Ypres, Belgium, and found a piece of stone that had been blown off the church there by the Germans during WWII, which he retained as a souvenir. Then he began collecting pieces from other buildings, like the Notre-Dame Cathedral in Paris, Edinburgh Castle, the Berlin Wall, the Great Wall of China, and even the Great Pyramid of Giza in Egypt. My personal favourite was a piece of limestone from 'Injun Joe's' cave, which Mark Twain wrote about. I'm not sure how McCormick and his entourage obtained these souvenirs,' but I'm going to cast a discreet veil over that. He had the architects Howells & Hood incorporate all of these parts and bobs into the building's front, and I must admit, they look wonderful, lurking in the heart of the "windy city." However, the place might have used a little Glasgow. Perhaps a piece of the original Duke of Wellington statue's plinth? With all the hoopla around the statue's regular capping, no one will notice; for more than forty years, people have climbed up to adorn the statue's head with an orange traffic cone. That's my hometown!

Aside from its architecture, two aspects of its history fascinate me: gangsterdom and, most importantly, the origin of rock 'n' roll. Gangsters in Chicago were a rare breed. In the 1920s, during the height of Prohibition, Al Capone ran his illegal gambling, bootlegging, and prostitution business from a fifth-floor bay window in the Lexington Hotel on South Michigan Avenue. Selling Moonshine' was simple: after his barrels of non-alcoholic booze were inspected by authorities, he had his men inject alcohol into them with large syringes, then sold the hard stuff in speakeasies, clandestine back-room bars with secret entrances that could be sealed off when the cops arrived. Scarface, nice little racket...

The Chicago blues were essential to the development of rock 'n' roll. There would have been no Led Zeppelin, Rolling Stones, or Allman Brothers; those legends rose to prominence by covering musicians like Muddy Waters, who were part of a musical scene that arose amid the great exodus of people leaving the southern states and travelling north. Thousands of African American men and women jumped on trains and packed into Chicago in the 1930s, bringing their music with them. Their acoustic guitars, violins, and harmonicas were electric in the clubs, and the entire scene quickly blossomed. I owe a great deal to rock 'n' roll. It has a wandering spirit at its core; it's about independence, adventure, and going your own way. It saved my life when I was a teenager. It arrived just when I was losing hope in my entire world - school, home, everything. Play 'Heartbreak Hotel' whenever you feel like you're a no-hoper. You'll realise you're not alone.

So, ever after my baby left me,

So, I've found a new location to live...

Rock 'n' roll was not the first musical genre to emerge in Chicago. I attended a service at the legendary Quinn Chapel, home to the United States' oldest black congregation, and heard the most amazing, moving, and dramatic gospel music. The Quinn Chapel was a gathering place for freed blacks, runaway slaves, and abolitionists, and it is considered one of the birthplaces of gospel music in America. The ceremony was full of remarkable spectacles, such as the preacher entering the church dressed as Jesus and carrying a massive cross on his back. My Catholic Masses as a child were nothing like that. I'd probably still be there if they had been. Instead of scaring us with hellfire, a few verses of 'Everybody's Gonna Have a Wonderful Time Up There' by Lee Roy Abernathy would have made all the difference. Those priests blew a golden opportunity back then. I could have been singing 'Doo Wop Doo Wop' while swinging the thurible. Before I left Chicago, I went to the top of the Willis Tower, previously the Sears Tower, which was the highest skyscraper in the world for twenty-five years, beginning in 1973. Views are spectacular. I stepped out into a little observation pod 110 stories up, firmly planted my cowboy boots on the glass floor, and peered down. Woooah. I don't mind heights in general, but this was the creepiest feeling. I could see the beginnings of Route 66 from this glassed-in crow's nest, the road I was going to journey 2,500 miles down, over eight states, right through the heart of America. I put on my leathers and chaps with the open crotch to keep my bollocks nice and aired, suitably orientated west. I hitched up, slipped on my helmet with the hidden microphone, and hopped on my tricycle. At the traffic lights, I talked to a few admirers, posed for some photos, and then I saw it: the sign that screamed 'ROUTE 66 BEGIN'. Yippee! But... wouldn't you think they'd add 'ROUTE 66 STARTS HERE'? However, it was more of a command: 'BEGIN!'

I started as instructed. I was driving towards Pontiac, my first major stop on America's most renowned highway, with cameras pointing at me from behind the automobile I was following. I felt like Peter Fonda in Easy Rider, and I was completely immersed in my Rambling Man persona. I knew I was heading into tornado territory, but the weather had been nice so far, and I was cruising easily towards my first pit stop: the Launching Pad restaurant, for a quick bite to eat. A 28-foot-tall plaster man in a green spacesuit towered above me on the roadway, carrying a rocket ship. 'Gemini the Giant' was one of the massive 'Muffler Men,' massive fibreglass statues that became tourist attractions across the United States. Gemini was purchased for $3,000 in 1965. It had to have been worthwhile. He could be seen for miles, so he was guaranteed to attract customers to the diner. There are many of these behemoths along Route 66. People had to do everything they could to entice people back to Route 66 after the Interstate Highway was created. That type of advertising, I'm sure, occurs all around the world. I once spotted a large sign that said, 'Stratford - home of New Zealand's only glockenspiel'. That took me by surprise. I assumed that every town would have one.

I adore all of the massive roadside attractions that can be found in the United States. A massive lobster lives near where I reside in the Florida Keys. And in LA, where I used to live, I used to love seeing the enormous doughnut, especially when it was raining, because it appeared to have been dunked. My road trip game became spotting other giants. I witnessed one create a shadow over the Palm Grill Café in Atlanta, Illinois, while dressed in blue pants and a red shirt and clutching a massive hot dog. Who the hell manufactures these things? Someone with a large studio, a large ladder, and a fear of heights. Bill Thomas, the café's owner, offered me a sample of one of his award-winning pies. I chose the peach. Delicious. I wish I could recall where I saw the massive banjo; I'd like to return for another quick look.

I said my goodbyes to Gemini and rode on to Godley, an old coal-mining town on the Will and Grundy County boundaries. A railway line used to straddle the border between the two counties, and in the 1930s, the proprietors of a local brothel created an amazing setup - they installed it inside a railway carriage! When the police arrived to perform a raid, everyone jumped out of bed and pushed the carriage across the county line to the next county, where the arriving officials had no jurisdiction. I'm laughing just thinking about that scene. I adore it when sex workers and bare-assed clientele all push the 'house of bad repute' aside to avoid charges. 'Put your back into it, Tiffany!' yelled the madam.

In Springfield, Illinois's state capital, I visited a residence once owned by President Abraham Lincoln. I discovered that Abe had a lot of options when it comes to taking a piss. There were three wooden toilet pots in his home's outhouse: a small, a medium, and a large. I busted out laughing because I imagined him sitting on one of those pots wearing his enormous hat. I also went inside his bedroom, where the wallpaper his wife had picked was obscenely 'busy' - a brown and beige leafy design over tree-trunk-like figures with accents of blue on a cream background. It was dreadful. I'd get seasick in my bed if Pamela put that at our house. But walking throughout Lincoln's house, touching items he touched and seeing where he sat to write, gave me a good feeling. People who lived in the region at the time recounted seeing him wheeling his children about in a cart, which was regarded quite unmanly at the time. That's admirable of him. When I used to push my own children around in a double stroller, some folks thought I was strange as well. But Rambling Men don't give a damn what other people think of us. 'Fuck the begrudgers!' we exclaim.

St Louis is the most populous city along Route 66, and it is here that I stepped inside the renowned Gateway Arch. It's an homage to the famous hunters and explorers of the West, made of nine hundred tons of stainless steel and hollow on the inside. I rode to the top of its cantilevered tramway and stood on a platform to gaze out over the Mississippi River, which was teeming with riverboats I'd only seen in movies. Unfortunately, no one ever asked me to spell M-I double-S-I double-S-I double-P-I, which was a huge letdown. When I was a boy, my sister Florence and several teachers attempted to hammer it into me for years with no pay-off.

St. Louis is not only the Gateway to the West, but it is also the birthplace of the most exquisite creature comfort: jogger bidets. 'Whaaaa? 'I believe you're joking, Bill!' I get what you're saying. Yes, in some ways, I am. In the city centre, there is a fountain with a runner dashing over water jets. I believe actual bidets for joggers are on the horizon, however slowing down in the middle of a marathon for a fast swish of your bollocks might be a bit of a nuisance... You'd need to have a crew ready to provide you with the wire brush and Dettol.

Before leaving St Louis, I saw a portion of a historical re-enactment of the American Civil War to commemorate the 150th anniversary. For months, hundreds of people had been rehearsing the Battle of Blackwell, dressed in mediaeval costumes and armed with rifles and cannons. They did a decent job of it. The Confederates triumphed that afternoon, but they were a little short on guys willing to pretend dead for three hours - with the exception of one guy with a nasty hangover. He voluntarily 'died' face up and slept until it was time to go home.

Remember how I said that people who owned businesses along Route 66 had to do everything they could to attract tourists? In Stanton, I went to the Meramec Caverns, which advertised itself as the hideout of outlaw Jesse James, though there are some doubts about that. It's a real cave, with several levels and lovely formations, and it's served many functions over the years. According to a Native American legend of the Osage tribe, the tribe took refuge there from extreme weather. It was mined for over a century after it was discovered to contain deposits of saltpetre, a key ingredient in gunpowder. People from Stanton even held summer dance parties in the cave because it had a nice, cool 'ballroom' in the 1890s. Wonderful concept! There were also plenty of dark corners for a quick kissipoo if the mood struck.

I came across another Route 66 giant in the town of Fanning. This time, it was a massive rocking chair. I ascended and sat on it. I was itching to rock back and forth, but the guy who built it informed me that the rockers, despite being 32 feet long, do not move. Pish, bah poo... I was distraught.

The true cowboy states are Oklahoma, Texas, New Mexico, and Arizona. They had the kinds of Route 66 landscapes I'd imagined before I came - long, straight roads that stretched as far as the eye could see and huge skies. It's ideal for biking. I passed the Midpoint Café and continued west, where I came across some truly isolated towns, many of which had been cut off by the construction of the Interstate Highway. 'We were raped,' Angel, also known as 'The Godfather of Route 66,' said. He'd seen a lot of changes in his eighty-four years. He remembered the 'dust bowl days,' when the route was a dirt road, and he'd seen local boys go off to World War II... and he was furious. 'When the Interstate Highway opened in 1978, we ceased to exist,' he explained. The state simply ignored us. There were no longer any signs.' He'd spent years campaigning for Route 66 to be designated as a historic route.

I can't imagine what it must have been like for locals when the Interstate Highway was built. In some cases, it happened quickly and without warning. People who relied on passing traffic for their businesses' success must have been devastated. When the new highway bypassed Glenrio in 1973, everyone left except for Roxanne, a woman I met whose father owned a gas station. She remained with her dogs because it was her home. Roxanne rose through the ranks to become mayor, sheriff, and everything else. There were no stores or services nearby after the mass exodus. For a pint of milk, she had to travel forty miles.

I was driving 300 miles from Payson, Arizona, and thought I was on the home stretch when I arrived in Albuquerque, New Mexico. The weather was beautiful, and the roads were straight and smooth. Maybe I became overconfident, because the next thing I knew, I was in the hospital with a busted knee and a broken rib. My throttle had become stuck on cruise control, and I had lost control of my motorcycle. When I hit the ground, I spun out, somersaulted, and broke a rib. Fortunately, some brilliant paramedics arrived on time. They really impressed me. Three of the five were motorcycle riders, and they carefully cut up the seams to remove my leather jacket so that it could be repaired later. It wasn't long before I was high on pain relievers and on the mend.

That wasn't the first time I'd gone off. I've had a lot of injuries on the road over the years, but a Rambling Man accepts that accidents or unpleasant events are unavoidable no matter how he travels. When he's on foot, the weather can make him very uncomfortable, he can trip and fall, he can be attacked by an animal or a human... The same logic applies to motorcycles: there will be an emergency, you will have to slam on your brakes, and you will end up on your arse. It's all part of the job. There is an understanding that it is not a car. There is no radio in it. It does not have a heating system. It's unpleasant to be outside in the rain. And that is how it is. Become accustomed to it. It's fine. I now live in Florida, where it is illegal to teach children anything - even Mark Twain is forbidden. Thank goodness, the Brooklyn Public Library offers free digital access to all banned books. They give out digital library cards so that you can access them from anywhere in the United States. Although Floridians are not permitted to read Mark Twain, they are permitted to ride motorcycles without a helmet or shoes. That is terrifying, in my opinion. Your helmet is essential. I know it's thrilling to ride without one, like standing at the bow of a ship with the wind rushing past your ears, but it's also deadly dangerous. You should also wear goggles to protect your eyes and something over your mouth to prevent you from swallowing hordes of insects... unless you're hungry for some wee, crunchy snacks. Many modes of transportation are hazardous, but the point is that they get you where you want to go. You take the necessary precautions and then proceed. You don't look too closely at it because overthinking certain things is what you gave up to become a Rambling Man.

Spending time with the Amish, just south of Springfield, was one of my favourite Route 66 experiences. I knew very little about them - a persecuted religious sect forced to flee nineteenth-century Europe and now living in self-exile - but they were lovely. They turned out to be completely different from what I had anticipated. I expected them to be stiff and prudish with their religion, 'holier-than-thou' and self-righteous, but they were the polar opposite. They wore their religion as easily as they wore their clothes. I stayed in a nearby Amish motel, but we ate at people's homes. Their food was delicious, with meat and potatoes and a cake and custard for dessert. It tasted like school dinner, which is my favourite type of food. The motel had electricity, but they still used gas lamps. They create the most amazing furniture. And they can laugh at themselves. Mervin, a guy I met, took me out in his horse and cart. I noticed his hat on a chair beside the door as we were leaving the house. 'Oh, you gotta wear the hat or I'm not coming!' I said. He simply replied, 'Sure!' and put it on. He told me about some Amish rules, such as not allowing pockets on shirts, and we were told not to point the camera too much at his face because it might encourage vanity.

Mervin let me drive his buggy, and as we drove through fields of wildflowers, I asked, 'Where did you meet your wife?' He smiled and said, 'Oh, I was probably somewhere I shouldn't have been.' He then proceeded to tell me about a farm accident he'd had years before. He had reversed over his fourteen-month-old daughter while moving a bale of hay, and she had died. Hearing him talk about it was extremely moving.

Learning about other people's lives enriches the life of a Rambling Man. Being in the company of Amish people taught me a valuable lesson. We stopped at a big McDonald's on the way out of Pennsylvania, and there was an Amish family standing around outside, looking awkward. They were being sniggered at. Normally, I would have simply walked away, but this time I approached the Amish family and stated, 'We just spent some time with some of your brothers and sisters, and we had a lovely time...' Amish people, like everyone else, want to be able to live their lives the way they believe they should be lived.

CHAPTER 2
I'D RATHER BUILD A BOAT THAN SAIL IN ONE

CALL ME OLD-FASHIONED, but aren't all boats nothing more than prisons with the option of drowning? Although I dislike sea travel, I occasionally fantasise about sailing from London to New York on one of the Queens. Seeing those massive ships makes me proud of Glasgow's shipyards. When Pamela and I went to see the Queen Mary in Los Angeles, I just stood there admiring the riveting and beautiful woodwork done by Clyde men. True artists. There were so many brilliant men with incredible traditional skills in those shipyards. They did amazing things with their hands, especially the woodworkers, joiners, and carpenters. The carving and fretwork on the furniture, as well as the precision of the joints and the perfectly finished claw and ball feet, were breathtaking.

I was fortunate to join the shipyards in the late 1950s and early 1960s, when they were still thriving. There were so many great tradesmen still working there, and we looked up to them. On one ship, I recall an opening from the engine to the propeller shaft that was welded both inside and outside. I was only an apprentice helping out nearby when a master welder approached me and said, 'C'mere. Take a look at that!' He pointed out all of the finished welding inside and outside the doorway, which was nothing short of miraculous. 'That's how good you have to be,' he said. The older men would frequently mock us apprentices, but they also inspired us. Encouraged us to be good at our jobs and to be proud of them.

That all changed after I completed my apprenticeship and became a full-fledged welder. At the time, the older men would always tell you that you were garbage, especially if you got a coveted job like working on the hull. You'd be busy overhead welding on the ship's keel, balanced on a plank, when someone would walk by and ask, 'How are you doing?' 'Okay, how are you?' you'd say. 'That's fucking crap,' they'd say when they saw your work. You must do better than that.' 'Be quiet.' They were always picking on you, but they knew you had to be good because you worked on the hull.

When I think back on the men I worked with in the Glasgow shipyards, I realise how many of them were Rambling Men at heart, but they were caught in a cycle of needing money to support not only their families, but also their drinking habits. I would have been the same if it hadn't been for my banjo, my dream of becoming a folk singer, and the courage to leave when I did. Willie McInnes, nicknamed 'Bugsy' due to his protruding two front teeth, gave me the push I needed to get out of the shipyards. Willie chastised me. 'What are you going to do with yourself?' he asked one day. 'What are you going to do with your banjo playing?' He himself was a guitarist. 'I'm going to quit and join the band and travel,' I said. 'When are you doing this?' he asked. 'When the holidays begin,' I said. Summer vacation was two or three months away. 'No, you're not,' he said. 'What do you mean, no I'm not?' I asked. 'You're putting it off,' he said. It's all a dream. If you really wanted to, you'd do it right now.' Well, I didn't do it right away, but what he said stayed with me. 'There's nothing worse than seeing someone who knows they could have gotten away and didn't do it,' he continued. It's as if they're locked up.' When summer vacation arrived and I received my vacation pay, I left and never returned. It took a leap of faith for me to pursue my dream of becoming a folk singer, but it was also the moment I fully surrendered to the life of a true Rambling Man.

I grew up on one side of the Clyde and went to school on the other, so I had to take the ferry across. Those ferries were fantastic. They were small boats piloted by Highlanders who would always say, 'Mind yer feet now, mind yer feet!' as you stepped off. As I sailed down the Clyde, I could hear all the welders, riveters, and caulkers at work in the shipyards. Some of them could even be seen from the ferry. And all the great liners would be sailing in and out - the three-funnelled ships of the Scottish Anchor Line fleet of merchant ships, as well as many other great ships. They'd be registered in Baltimore, Tierra del Fuego, or Rio de Janeiro, fly different flags, and have different coloured funnels. I was always saying to myself, 'One day, I'll go to the Middle East,' or 'One day, I'll go to Shanghai and Hong Kong.' I was desperate to get to the sea. That was the Rambling Man spirit in me when I was younger.

Those ferry rides to school were proof, and a constant reminder, that there was a big wide world out there waiting to be explored, or drunk in. I've seen a lot of the big world now. In fact, I tell my children that I've ruled the world like a colossal colossus. If my plan to flee to the sea had succeeded, I would have seen even more. In Glasgow, there was a place called The Pool where you could join the merchant navy. My father caught me going there twice and dragged me back to finish my apprenticeship.

Other ferries around Glasgow and the Scottish Isles were also enjoyable. With a black and white hull and a red, white, and black funnel, the PS Waverley is a well-known ferry. It is a classic seagoing passenger-carrying paddle steamer - the world's last of its kind. Everyone enjoys it. It reminds them of their childhood Clyde. My favourite paddle steamer, however, was the Jeanie Deans. She was built in Govan on the Clyde in 1931, and I used to sail her to Rothesay when I went on vacation with my family. The trip took about an hour, and we stopped at Dunoon along the way, where some people got off. The Meikles, who lived through the wall in our tenement building, used to go to Dunoon - back then, people had a habit of returning to the same vacation spot year after year. My father would take me down to see the engine once the ferry was underway. It was in a huge, noisy room filled with painted piping, gleaming metal, and all sorts of things whirring and clunking away. It was a very happy occasion. There was a small café on board that served meat pies and tea, and there were people on deck singing nostalgic songs and playing accordion and fiddle. After falling in love with the ferries in Glasgow, I began to appreciate them wherever I went. In New Zealand, I sailed on several. I boarded the Arahura ferry ship with my trike, which travels from Picton on the South Island to Wellington on the North Island. It's my favourite New Zealand ferry ride because the scenery reminds me of the Clyde. I also took a ferry from Auckland to Waiheke Island, which is only forty minutes away in the Hauraki Gulf. There are wineries, native forests, and waterfalls, as well as a fantastic sculpture walk with life-size corrugated iron cows. I contacted the artist and purchased an iron cow for my Scottish home. I sent it to 'graze' in a field behind my house, which confused my Highland cattle.

A Rambling Man is drawn to anything that gets you from point A to point B, and ferries are frequently used because they are so convenient. You'll eventually come to a water's edge if you walk far enough, so you'll have to take the ferry across to discover new land, another adventure. It's a simple way to connect two long walks. Aside from convenience, ferries can provide spectacular views and be very entertaining. The traditional, large green and yellow ferries that plough their way across Sydney Harbour from Circular Quay in Australia pass the pearly sails of the Sydney Opera House, go under the Sydney Harbour Bridge, and glide past the colourful, smiling jaws of Luna Park, onwards to the shoreline towns. It's fantastic. During one of my British tours, I sailed up the River Thames to my performance at the New Globe Theatre, passing the massive sightseers' Ferris wheel known as the London Eye. Even though the docklands have been revitalised with trendy restaurants and office buildings, the same old smells remain. Rope, wood, and whisky are instantly recognizable. Maybe the whisky smells better in the Glasgow docks, but it was all very familiar to me.

I thought the New Globe was fantastic. The setting is identical to Shakespeare's open-air theatre, and performing there was a pleasure. Everyone was nervous because it was just a few days after 9/11. When an aeroplane flew overhead while I was onstage, the mood of the audience instantly changed. 'Don't move!' I said sternly as I pulled my T-shirt up over my head like a balaclava. People will crowd around you, stealing your expensive jewellery...' People screamed with laughter - it seemed like a huge release, as if it lifted the curse of all that accumulated fear. After my concert, I spoke with some actors who had been in the audience, and they told me how lucky I was to be able to say such things spontaneously. When they were onstage and something unusual occurred in the theatre, they were always forced to stick to the script, no matter how much they wanted to say something different.

The New Globe's mediaeval design is ideal for a comedian. Everyone in the audience seemed to be standing close to me. People in the narrow upper galleries, on the other hand, were not very comfortable because their knees were constricted. People must have been shorter in Elizabethan times... I had a good laugh with them about it. But I liked having people standing right next to the stage in the pit. They were known as stinkards' during Shakespeare's time because they farted a lot and generally smelled bad.

I believe that the best parts of many cities are often the waterside areas. In Auckland, New Zealand, I enjoy being near the harbour. Pamela was born nearby, and she has a large number of Mori relatives. Her Uncle Bill once showed me around. He took me on a tour of the dock, and I got to see all of the big yachts. New

Zealanders love yachting and seafaring, and they're very good at it. On Saturdays, they go sailing. It was beautiful to see all of the white sails out on the harbour. They also compete in races. I've never been anywhere where that was a typical Saturday activity. There will be no drinking, football, or pub brawls; just a lot of fun on the ocean waves. The Henley-on-Todd Regatta is a very different type of boat race held near Alice Springs, Australia. Australians are notoriously irreverent, so it's no surprise that they devised a spoof of the famous posh regatta at Henley-on-Thames in the United Kingdom. There is one major difference, however: there is no water in the Todd River, so they simply cut the arse out of their boats and set sail. Then, eight to ten people climb into each boat, hold up the sides, and run along the sandy dry riverbed. It's supposed to be an annual event, but when it rains, the fun is ruined and the boat race has to be cancelled because the river fills up. That kind of nonsense makes me happy. The tranquillity of travelling by barge on the British canals appeals to me. During one of my British tours, I took a trip that began near Sheffield and ended in London. Canals are brilliant in their own right. They're not tidal, and they don't get churned up in storms. Going up the canal on a barge called Milly Molly Mandy made me feel a little less than manly. I could have gone with Discovery or Pathfinder if I wanted something with more rawhide and moccasins. Mandy, Milly, Molly! I should have been dressed in pyjamas with feet.

Despite the fact that I've had some wonderful trips on the water, mostly for the purpose of catching things that were once perfectly happy, If I had to choose between swimming in the deep and sailing in one, I'd rather build a boat. That may not make sense to everyone, but it's part of being a Rambling Man, because a Rambling Man enjoys making things. Whether it's carrying a banjo around and playing music, disassembling and reassembling your motorcycle, learning how to build something from nothing, or painting a beautiful picture, the process of creating something is what he enjoys the most. He is perfectly content with impermanence and can take or leave the finished product.

And, as I previously stated, once on a boat, you're stuck there until you reach your destination, which can be difficult if you're a restless person. But if you're in a boat and fishing, that's fine. I enjoy fishing. I'm willing to fish anywhere, on land or in the water. I caught an

Australian salmon in New South Wales. On the beach, my fishing guide and I were the only ones. It was a dream come true. At the time, some kids were surfing in the ocean. When I was a kid, no one knew what surfing was. 'Oh, look! There's a man on an ironing board in the sea.' In any case, attempting to surf or windsurf in Scotland would have resulted in fucking hypothermia. But did you know that windsurfing dates back to the Victorian era in Scotland? We invented it, and I can prove it: in the film Mrs Brown, with its very authentic depictions of Victorian times, there's a scene where I've just finished swimming and come out of the sea. I'm drying off and talking to my brother, and if you look closely, you can see a windsurfer in the background behind his head.

Some Australians use fish as bait to catch worms. 'When would fish be used for catching worms?' Answer: In some parts of Australia, they mash up dead fish and stuff them into the leg of a woman's nylon stocking, which they then dangle over incoming waves to attract six to twelve inch long worms. When one of them raises its head above the surface of the water, you use a credit card to trap its head against your fingernail and pull it out. I enjoyed fishing in Darwin, Australia's northernmost city. A large storm loomed on the horizon in one part of the sky, which was blue with white fluffy clouds. Nature showing you how insignificant you are was a dramatic and beautiful thing, and it was very, very good for you. I caught a small barramundi between the sun and the storm. It was the perfect size for a frying pan. My favourite fish in the world is most likely barramundi. It has the same appearance as salmon but tastes better. It tastes even better than haddock, which is saying a lot. A red dragonfly landed beside me as I was fishing for barramundi. I didn't move a single muscle. I didn't flinch, cry, or run for cover. I didn't even get my pants wet. Because that is what I am.

My father used to say that thunder was God rearranging his furniture. In Australia, you have the best thunderstorms. It's wonderful to lie in bed and gaze out at the sky theatre. Yippee! The sky is strewn with incredible colours at sunset in the Australian outback. It looks like a bad painting at times, like one of those velvet jobs with birds sitting on a burnt tree stump, all in silhouette. Extraordinary gold and black tones. The place resembles a fridge magnet. It's magnificent. Some days, you're glad you were born.

I enjoy fishing the Green River in Utah, USA, as well as other locations, but the best fishing I've ever had was in New Zealand. Rainbow trout are indigenous to North America, while brown trout are indigenous to the United Kingdom, and New Zealanders imported both varieties. They thrived, thankfully, without becoming a nuisance. In Christchurch, trout can be seen swimming through the city centre. That city has undergone significant transformations in recent years. The earthquakes took care of that. I've never been in a major earthquake, but when I was bathing one of my little girls in Los Angeles, there was a massive aftershock. A wave smashed into the bath - shoom! Fuck! Amy, who was six years old at the time, replied, 'Four point five.' And she was correct!

In 2011, a major earthquake struck Christchurch. The town was beautiful before the disaster, but after 'the big one,' everything was rebuilt at a lower elevation. Instead of multi-story malls, there were lots of small wooden shops with sheltered pathways outside - a completely different feel to the town that I really like. There, I met a Scotsman who was a dentist with a passion for fishing. 'You like to fish, don't you?' he asked. And I replied, "Yeah." 'You have to come here and fish,' he said. You each get a loach.' He wasn't joking. If you arrive at a loch and someone is already casting there, you say, 'Okay, I'll go to the next one.' Fishing comes naturally to a Rambling Man. It's free food, and you can set up your rod anywhere in the world. It's just you, the water, and whatever is swimming around in it. It's fine to bring a friend as long as they understand the rules: talk quietly and don't disturb the fish.

I used to go there to catch tarpon years before I moved to the Florida Keys. I enjoy fishing off the coasts of Key West and Sugarloaf Key. Some of the locals catch fish while standing on their paddleboards. Not with this soldier. I also enjoyed a fishing lodge in Tulum, Mexico. It's a simple wooden structure on the beach with about six lodges that serve delicious Mexican food. Jamie, my son, and I went there. We'd get up early and go out on the boat with a guide, then return at night for dinner. There was enough room on the boat to stand up and fly-fish in the shallows of the sea, which are about six feet deep and home to bonefish, tarpon, and permit. I normally release fish after catching them, but one of my fellow guests in Mexico was offended. 'I've never understood the concept of catching fish with all that special equipment and clothing and special flies -

then letting it go,' he said. The owner of the fishing lodge stepped in. 'Do you participate in any sports yourself?' he inquired of the visitor. 'Yeah,' he replied, 'Tennis.' 'When the game is over, do you eat the ball?' inquired the owner.

Of course, I have many favourite fishing spots in Scotland; catching a small trout or salmon in the Highlands is a joy. When I went to buy some flies, an elderly Highlander was sitting there making some stunning patterns. He gave me a beautiful fly he'd just made. 'I'll give you some advice,' he said. Get out of the river while you're typing this on your line. Turn your back and hide behind a tree; otherwise, the salmon will grab it from your grasp!'

I used to spend the day fishing with my friend Jimmy Kent. We'd look for the ideal location, and you usually know which rivers to visit based on their appearance - salmon rivers, for example, are dark and swirly, whereas trout rivers are browner. Nothing beats the weight of the water pressing against your legs and the wee birds singing away... it's brilliant. You're breathing the purest air up there, right up your nose, straight from the water. When you go salmon fishing in Scotland, the weather is always perfect: howling gale, blazing sunshine, snow, occasional rain, soggy underfoot or very dry - it's going to be a fantastic day! You must be prepared for any weather. I was fishing in a Scottish stream once and came out of the water cold. As I was packing my belongings, I noticed a small Glasgow man walking by. I was wearing a Glengarry Highland bonnet, just to be windswept and interesting, and he was wearing brand-new plus fours in a strange blue that doesn't exist in nature, with socks to match. He was a shambles, but he had the audacity to tell me, 'If I had a hat like that, I wouldn't fucking wear it.'

Tasmania has fantastic trout, and the people are wonderful. Country people with a very modern attitude. No, not at all. I made the front cover of a Tasmanian fishing magazine because I caught the same fish twice in two days. I almost caught it, but it escaped. I caught it the next day, and it still had the fly in its mouth from the day before. As a result, I became quite well-known among Tasmanian anglers. Fishing in the warmer seas and rivers of Australia, New Zealand, Mexico, and Florida is a welcome relief. My bollocks can only take so much freezing water.

At home, I have an outside shower that is supposed to be very healthy. There's a bit of a jungle growing around three sides of it, so I feel like I'm scrubbing myself in the Amazon. It's fantastic. I do, however, check under the leaves first to see if there's anything creeping around. The only other outdoor bathing experience I've had that compares is in Rotorua, a fascinating geothermal town in New Zealand where two tectonic plates collide. It was very pleasant to lie in a natural thermal spring like it was a bath. I was wearing a hairy possum swimming costume at the time. I couldn't pass it up when I saw it in a store. After purchasing it, the only place to wear it was in the water, because you can't walk around on the grass while wearing a furry costume. My pubic hair appeared to be out of control as I lay in that warm, sulphur bath. However, it was a very enjoyable aquatic experience. Pamela's birthday gift of one hour in an isolation tank was also memorable. It was as if I had jumped into a tin of boot polish. I could have had a quick fifty off the wrist in there, but I was afraid someone was watching on video.

When I was in the Arctic, I wanted to catch fish, but there was nothing available. There is, however, a creature with the unfortunate name of 'ugly fish'. Appropriately named. It's enormous, with a tiny tail and a huge fucking ugly head resembling a giant wart. The only edible part is the arse, which is located just before the tail. Imagine being called 'ugly' your entire life, and your best feature is your arse!

The best sea voyage I've ever taken was one that has tested sailors and navigators for centuries. I was filming a TV show called Journey to the Edge of the World in which I travelled from the Atlantic Ocean to the Pacific Ocean the hard way: 10,000 miles across the top of the world via the fabled "Northwest Passage." It was a fantastic adventure, and I'm glad I got to participate in it. For centuries, it was ice-bound all year and no one could get through, but with recent melting, there are a few weeks in the summer when you can travel through. It was a perilous journey straight out of the Call of the Wild novels that had inspired my childhood adventure fantasies. I visited some desolate locations.

I began in Iqaluit, which is located in the Canadian territory of Nunavut. I'd arrived just in time for lunch, which was Muktuk - beluga soup - with a caribou burger for a main course. That was my first indication that I wasn't in Kansas anymore. Suitably fortified, I flew over the icebergs to Baffin Island, which is home to an Inuit community. Most of the year, the area is blanketed in snow. When you look around, everything is white, but as the snow melts, you can see all the things that are just lying around outside the stores and people's houses, and you think to yourself, 'The white was nice.' 'Road to Nowhere' is written on a sign just outside the township. It's no surprise that the area is popular among courting couples. It reminded me of when my kids would come home late at night and when I asked, 'Where were you?' they'd say, 'Uh...nowhere.' I've noticed that The Office bars can be found in many American cities. The concept is the same. I then flew 180 miles north to Pangnirtung, an old whaling town on the Cumberland Sound's shores. The Hudson's Bay Company used it as a trading post with the local Inuit. Whalers exported whale oil, and it was a massive industry until the whale population began to decline. I was taken aback when I met an Inuit man who played Scottish music on an accordion. He purchased the instrument from Hudson's Bay Company in 1973. When the town was thriving, Scottish whalers spent the winters here, bringing their music and instruments with them. Every country in the world has a Scot or two. We're a country of Rambling Men. As I began my journey to Iyaituk National Park, I crossed the Arctic Circle. Snowfields, tundra plains, ice flows, and mountains towering above me were all perfectly reflected in shining, clear lakes. I'd been told this was polar bear territory and was hoping for a rifle to protect myself. Unfortunately, all they did was teach me how to use bear spray. I strode out into the wilderness, armed with my trusty aerosol... and fell on my arse crossing a freezing stream. It was unusually quiet. A sense of vast emptiness. As I climbed into my tent that night, I said to myself, "Goodnight, my dear and sweet repose." You won't squash your nose if you lie on your back. I just added my own twist: And keep your bear spray close at hand.

The next day, we flew over incredible fiords and the 2,500-square-mile Turner Glacier in a helicopter. It is currently melting due to global warming and making a lot of noise while doing so. Later that day, I met Abraham, an Inuit elder with a laugh that sounded eerily similar to that melting glacier. I started to feel like I was on another planet, albeit a stunningly beautiful one. On Igloolik Island, deep inside the Arctic Circle, people still live in traditional ways. You know how people in the UK say things like, 'The wind was Arctic...' They have no idea, to be honest. My London-purchased winter jacket was deemed inadequate for the Arctic temperatures, so I had to be fitted for a made-to-measure sealskin suit. The woman who made it used the kitchen floor tiles to measure my feet. She talked while measuring my entire body, saying a lot of things I didn't understand. However, I believe she said, 'You have wonderful manly arms that could kill a caribou with one squeeze.' At the very least, I could probably scare an animal to death by leaping from behind a tree dressed like that.

I sailed around a few icebergs to Igloolik Point, a historic ceremonial site. Captain William Parry and his men were iced in here in 1822 while on an expedition to find the Northwest Passage. When one of the crew members began seeing a local married woman, all hell broke loose. The town's headman asked the local shaman to cast a spell to get rid of the sailors, and the ice broke the next day, according to legend. Although Parry's men set sail, a 36-year-old man named Alexander Elder did not survive the winter of 1823. They broke ten pickaxes while digging his grave. It's no surprise that the Inuit didn't bother burying people, instead dumping them on an iceberg.

The Northwest Passage terminates at Pond Inlet on the north coast. The icy wilderness there is incredible. It's the harshest place I've ever seen. I went grouse hunting in the area, but it was a long way from tiptoeing across the moors to bagging a few grouse. I felt guilty for being present during the seal hunt, despite the fact that seals are not an endangered species, there are 5 million in Arctic waters, and the Inuit eat them to survive. As I waited for a seal to pop his head up from the boat, I reminded myself that it was part of the culture. I was all for them continuing to do what they'd been doing for centuries and knew they needed to be allowed to kill their quota of animals, but I was still a bleeding-heart hippy liberal, and it was difficult to accept. In the Arctic, I learned a lot about myself and how the real world works. Some people go hunting, while others go to butchers.

Hundreds of people died while searching for the Northwest Passage. I was following in the footsteps of great Rambling Men, of pioneers and dreamers. I was meeting people who lived on the very edge of the world in the wilderness. That journey was mostly by ship, and I sailed 10,000 miles through the Arctic Ocean to reach Vancouver Island. It was supposed to be summer, but the weather station in Resolute Bay was bitterly cold. There was nothing but tundra - nothing grew there. It is extremely dangerous to fly there. I saw the wreckage of a Canadian Lancaster bomber, my all-time favourite plane. This one had crashed during a weather report run in 1950. Fortunately, only one person was hurt and no one died. In comparison, the first people to arrive there arrived by boat 100 years ago. The Tuli people, the Inuit's forefathers, travelled by sea from Alaska to Greenland. I saw the wreckage of their boat, which had a small lemming living inside beneath the whalebone arches.

I boarded a Russian cruise ship with a hundred other passengers for the next leg of my journey north. It was only the second cruise ship to visit the area in six years, and it was also my first cruise. First, we practised for "the unlikely event that the ship began sinking." We were all required to report to mustering stations and train for the end of our lives. 'Will we all fit in that wee lifeboat?' I inquired. 'Well, it'll be nice and cosy,' someone replied. 'Well, I'm just looking for who I'm most likely to eat if everything goes wrong,' I explained. Nobody replied. I'd obviously created an uneasy environment. The captain continued ominously over the loudspeaker, 'Next time this happens, it will be for real.' I proceeded to the bridge to speak with the captain. He described the ship as a Class B icebreaker. 'We won't be able to break the ice, but we can get around it.' That's useful to know.

Sir John Franklin, an explorer from the mid-nineteenth century, attempted but failed to find the Northwest Passage. The British knew it wasn't possible, but they sent him anyway, along with 129 men in two ships, none of whom were ever seen again. They became stranded on Beechey Island in the winter of 1845, where many of them died. I was supposed to land on that very island, but three polar bears had been spotted just before I arrived, and I wasn't about to step ashore with some hairy oaf waiting to scoff me. I could see from the ship that the area was desolate. Even though it was summer, it was awful and cold. John Torrington, one of Franklin's men, was buried there. A post-mortem was performed in 1984, and it was discovered that he died of lead poisoning from eating the canned food. Those men resembled astronauts. They were well-equipped. They had a library with 3,000 books on board their ship. There was also a carpentry shop, a blacksmith, and a shooting range on board. Even with all of that, I couldn't imagine being stuck in such a desolate place, wondering if you'd ever return home.

The colours I saw while cruising the Arctic Sea - the intense blues of the water and sky, the gleaming silvery-white of the ice - reminded me of a Disneyland theme park. It was beautiful to look at. But I'd think twice about coming here without sheepskin underwear, and I'd think twice even more if I didn't know if I could go home again. As we sailed further north, we discovered that ice was impeding our progress. We had to reroute because the wind had blown massive pieces into our path. I like how, even now, getting through the Northwest Passage isn't guaranteed. The captain attempted to summon an icebreaker, but none were available, so we charted a course through Peel Sound. We had the luxury of an ice chart, but I imagined what it would have been like without one, in a wooden square-rigged ship like Franklin's, with their tinned food killing them. We sailed to King William Island, where Franklin's men had established a camp after being forced to abandon their ships. In this frozen wasteland, one hundred and twenty-six despicable men died one by one. The Franklin Expedition came to an end at Victory Point, the most miserable place on Earth. Ten years later, search parties shocked Victorian Britain by reporting cannibalism evidence. It had to have been hell. This is not a sport for white linen pants and a picnic basket, I assure you.

Franklin discovered the Northwest Passage, according to a plaque in Westminster Abbey. He did not do so. A Norwegian named Roald Amundsen was the first to cross it 53 years after Franklin's disappearance, on a three-year journey from 1903 to 1906. He did everything correctly. He had a smaller ship with a shallow draft and a crew of only six people. He stopped on King William Island, learned the language, met the locals, dressed in furs, and researched the area. There are still people with Norwegian ancestry there, so the Norwegians must have had a few cuddles with the local women. Nonetheless, Amundsen stated that the best thing to do is to leave the Inuit alone to live their lives as they have always done. He navigated the entire way to Vancouver Island using local knowledge, but he couldn't have done so without a discovery made by a Scottish explorer named John Rae. Rae explored a southern route by dogsled that no one else would have been able to take. I believe we should dispatch a stonemason to Westminster Abbey to clear the air.

We finally made it through the Northwest Passage on our trusty cruise ship. After disembarking, I flew across the Arctic Ocean to

Tuktoyaktuk, an isolated community on the very edge of the continent. That is not a word to use with loose dentures. But the name of the people who live there is even more difficult to pronounce: TUKTUUYAQTUUMUKKABSI. Is it because they think they're Welsh? For the final leg of my journey, I hitched a ride on an ice truck along the Dempster Highway - an ice road - with a guy who regularly delivered fruit and vegetables over 5,000 miles round trip. I picked up a hitchhiker in Scotland many years ago who had the audacity to tell me he didn't like my comedy, so I pulled over and let him out. I was extremely cautious with what I said to Dan the driver there, on the blizzard-prone edge of the Arctic Circle. Later, I went hiking in the Tombstone Mountains with Lolita, a gun-toting woman. We hiked up to an unnamed lake. I proposed the name "Lake." Thank God - I Couldn't Take Another Step'. Do you think it'll fit on the road signs?

I eventually arrived in Dawson City, Canada's Yukon Territory. In 1896, George Cormack discovered gold near the confluence of the Yukon and Klondike rivers, a popular fishing spot for indigenous people who had lived there for thousands of years. It quickly became the world's hottest gold location. It was dubbed the Klondike gold rush. Dredgers were used by some to extract 50 pounds of gold per day. There is still gold mining there. I tried my hand at panning. It's hairy-chested men's work, and I can't say I enjoyed it - there's something about wet underwear that I've never found appealing. I'm a huge Jessie fan. My father used to refer to me as a 'Jessie' all the time. That means you're not manly and can't play football very well in Scotland. 'You're a big fucking Jessie!' he'd say. Years later, I was in Hawaii and came across a place called Jessie's. Pamela photographed me in the parking lot next to a sign that read, 'Parking for Jessie's Only,' and sent it to my father. Standing in the middle of breathtakingly beautiful countryside, I staked my own gold mining claim by sinking a post in the bush and naming it the "Billy Claim." I wish I had given it more thought. I squandered a once-in-a-lifetime opportunity to name it something more fuckyouish, like 'Don't Even Think About Panning Here Or BIG FURRY THINGS WILL BITE OFF YOUR BALLS!' No one can move that claim for the next hundred years, according to the law. I suppose I should go back and look a little harder for a wee nugget. However, it is not a region for Jessies. I had the worst night at the campfire because the guys kept talking about bears all night. I tried to sleep, but I was convinced that there was one nearby who would consider me a tasty dinner, so I didn't get a wink. The following day, I met the most impressive woman I'd ever met. Nancy is a true Rambling Man. She ran a wonderful ranch guesthouse near Telegraph Creek. Telegraph Creek used to be like Las Vegas, providing supplies and entertainment for visitors during three gold rushes, but it is now a ghost town. Nancy, who was five feet two inches tall and seventy-five years old, managed a 480-acre ranch on her own fifty miles down a dirt road. She was so assured and capable that I was convinced she had trapped grizzly bears and wrestled them to the ground. She took me out on her boat with an outboard motor, then drove me to the guesthouse in her tractor. Her driveway stretched for four miles. My$$ was busy making buttons. I was completely taken aback by her strength. I watched as she split logs for the winter with a single blow of her axe. She gutted moose on a regular basis and used her rifle to scare off wolves and bears. 'Once upon a time, I saw a bear coming down from the hills into my yard,' she explained. 'I knew the kids were playing outside, so I ran and got my rifle and shot it just as it was crossing the creek there,' says the shooter. Nancy was completely self-sufficient, and I admired her joy and energy. She showed me around her property. It was a beautiful location with breathtaking scenery. That night, she made me moose stew with cabbage and beans for dinner, followed by a cakey treat. I wanted to propose to her. When I got up to go to bed, I discovered a note she had left for me in my room. 'Hello!' I thought at first. She shares my sentiments!' But that wasn't the case. 'You must get some rest,' said the note. It is unpleasant to be cold. I recommend wearing warm nightwear and socks to bed.' This is the type of hotel I prefer. 'Don't you think this way of life could become too difficult for you?' I asked. She simply scoffed. 'I'm not a quitter,' she says.

It was almost time to return home, but first I had to travel 600 miles south to Gitlaxt'aamiks, a Native American settlement, for a traditional sweat lodge ritual. 'What does that entail?' I inquired. 'Oh, you're getting boiled and steamed.' They were not joking. A steam bath was created inside the sweat lodge by the intermittent pouring of water onto hot rocks. Aside from the glow of the red-hot lava rocks that turned white as they burned, it was pitch black. The sweat lodge was so hot at times that I felt like I was sitting on the inside of a volcano just before it erupted. There were five sessions, each hotter and more intense than the one before it. A girl once brought in frozen fruit in her Thermos. Eating the frozen fruit in the fire room was delicious.

While the temperature rose, people were saying prayers, chanting, and openly discussing various physical and emotional experiences. People believe that the ceremony cleanses you from the inside out. It eliminates negative energy and restores balance to your life. Another bucket of water was poured on the rocks, and a wave of hot steam rolled through the circle. The chanting became more intense. Everyone was sweating, but despite the fact that it tested my endurance, it felt peaceful. Some of the men spoke of being taken away by the authorities as children, happy children living in their culture. But the authorities insisted on transporting them to strange schools and homes across Canada, where their language and culture were beaten out of them. Their parents had had no say in the matter. They were not permitted to speak or eat in their native language. These grown men were sobbing in front of the fire because they missed their language and the company of their peers. They claimed it had all been stolen and would not be returned. Because of what had happened to him, a big muscular man was crying like a baby. It moved me deeply. I also said a few words. I admitted that I sometimes felt I wasn't grateful enough, that I didn't take enough time to appreciate my life, the people around me, and the world in general. It's difficult to explain why or how, but the sweat lodge had a significant impact on me. The next day, I cut down a tree in Horsefly, California. Leonard Cecil and his loggers dressed me up in orange clothes and a helmet and declared that I looked the part. We were supposed to cut down trees infested with the destructive pine beetle. It's a risky business. I'd started to become a rufty-tufty on my trip to the Arctic and through the Northwest Passage. When I left home, I was a nice tree-hugging hippy. I was afraid my wife would not recognize me in my new Grizzly Adams persona. That's what the wild outdoors does to you. 'Chainsaw cuts don't hurt,' Leonard says. 'I've had more painful shaving cuts.' His face was scarred, but I didn't want to ask which activity he was worse at: cutting down trees or shaving. He taught me how to use a chainsaw, and I cut down a large tree. Of course, I hugged it first. The sheer force with which it fell was incredible. That was quite a rush. I enjoy working with men's camaraderie, but I was disappointed that no one yelled 'Timberrrr!!!' And none of them were dressed in tartan - I was in tears. That long journey came to an end at Friendly Cove in the Pacific Ocean. I'd driven 10,000 miles in ten weeks. Captain Cook discovered Friendly Cove in 1776 while searching for the Northwest Passage. Cook had retired at the time, following his exploits in the Pacific Ocean, but a substantial prize of £20,000 had been offered to the first group through, so the British Admiralty decided Cook was their man. Cook, like many men before and after him, found nothing. The interior of a doughnut. It was an incredible journey for me. I'd had a once-in-a-lifetime opportunity to visit some extraordinary places during the Arctic summer. There were some wonderful people present. I'd never felt such helpfulness or welcome anywhere else. They were people who knew who they were and wouldn't want to live anywhere else. And I'll never forget the constant fear of polar bears, or the overwhelming sensation of being completely surrounded by water and ice. It was extremely humbling. Do we really understand the power of water as humans? In an English hotel, I took a hairdryer from its bag and noticed a small tag on it. I expected it to say "Return to the front desk." Don't even THINK about packing this, you big fucking long-haired oaf! And if I had your hair, I'd have my own fucking equipment.' But did you notice what it said? 'Do not use it in the shower. 'Who is this notice for?' I wondered.

CHAPTER 3
STRUCK BY LIGHTNING

I'M NOT VERY VOCAL ABOUT MY SEX LIFE; I'M JUST GRATEFUL. 'AHHHH!' I've been known to scream in other situations, such as on an aeroplane when it takes a downward turn halfway across the Atlantic Ocean and feels like it's plummeting seaward... But that kind of soiled-trousers panicking is long gone. I stopped being afraid of flying after realising that if the plane crashes at cruising altitude, you won't feel anything. You can relax once you're above maiming height. It's natural to be nervous when flying. Every creature on Earth feels the same way. I noticed two caterpillars observing a butterfly. 'You'll never get me up on one of those things,' one said to the other. On the contrary, I enjoy being up high. It's just the idea of plummeting to your death that bothers me. I've never had vertigo, probably because I grew up working on suspended planks in shipyards. And when I was a teenager apprentice welder, I survived a massive fall from the deck of a ship. They called me 'Lucky Bill' after that. I used to have reverse vertigo, which means that when you're not high, you're scared. New Zealanders appear to be experts at jumping from great heights. I skydived off the tallest building in the southern hemisphere in Auckland. I felt stupid, though, because despite being in the parachute regiment, I landed like a bundle of laundry. Kersplat! 'Owww! Fer Pete's sake...!!!' Although times change, standards should not. I discovered one of the best laxatives known to man in Queenstown, New Zealand: bungee jumping from a suspended platform into a gorge. And I did it while naked. I entered a sturdy structure perched above a gorge. The people who ran the jump greeted me at the door and showed me where I could leave my clothes. I was then forced to walk naked into a larger room with about a dozen other people, some of whom worked there, but others who were simply relatives who'd come because they were nosy. There was a lovely little blond boy with Down syndrome. He had a lovely face. 'Hello!' he said. I introduced myself as 'Hello!' 'Where are your clothes?' he asked. 'Over there,' I said. I like to jump around naked.' He said: 'Why?' 'I dunno,' I said, and he laughed. I went through the outer door, then down a passageway to a narrow platform that looked like a diving board. They put the equipment on me there. It was a harness with webbed straps and buckles, as well as two straps that came up the side of your thighs and around your waist, similar to parachute gear. I was told to proceed forward to where the platform widened slightly. I was standing on this twelve-inch square platform, thinking to myself, 'I hope I don't fall!', which made no sense because I was about to fall anyway. They then told me to wait a few moments until I was ready, then tip myself forward. There was no shoving or machinery. It was completely silent. Very holy. It's just you and the rest of the world. You fall for a long time, feeling the wind rush past your face. As you fall, you can see all of the mountains and trees. I remember seeing a group of large boulders coming towards me - because I was leading with my face - and thinking: 'This wasn't such a great plan. Billy, that's not the brightest idea you've ever had.' But then I started to like it. I eventually felt a 'give' as the line reached its length, and it wheeked me back up in the air. 'Eeehhh!!!' I bounced a couple of times. That was a wonderful sensation. Freedom. The line then became slack. After that, you hold on to the rope while they slowly raise you, and you can simply step back onto the platform when you're level with it.

However, when I returned to the platform, I felt as if I'd told a dirty joke to nuns because I was naked and they weren't. When the filming was finished, the charm and bravery faded, and I felt like a naked guy flaunting his body. Everyone in the room wanted me to sign their photos, books, and albums, but I said, "You'll have to excuse me - I feel awkward." 'I'd like to put my clothes back on.' I could tell some of them were looking at my willy, so I just stared back. 'Yes? 'Can I assist you?

Flying in an aeroplane is a piece of cake compared to bungee jumping, though I'm terrified of the airport's moving floor. I've decided to walk alongside it. I've been trying for years to get on one of them without looking like a jerk. Most people do it flawlessly. They simply walk on while conversing with someone. 'Aye, Bobby, aye...' and they're off. Maybe I think about it too much. I try to slow down as I approach it, which usually results in me tripping. Lurching. It truly degrades one's dignity. When you lurch, your elbows may come up. You didn't ask them to do it; it just happens. You even make a little noise now and then. 'Oou Ughhhh!' comes a small, surprised exclamation. I'm sure there are guys controlling those things in a room somewhere. They're watching their video monitor and notice you approaching. 'Oh, there is one!' 'Willie, that was a cracker - she grabbed the wean, hahah!' 'He smashed his take-out right there!' Bastards. 'Make the bannister move faster, Bobby...' 'You bastard!' The only way to avoid embarrassment is to pretend you intended to lurch. But that means doing the entire journey in this manner. Another flying embarrassment is sleeping with your mouth wide open, and occasionally your tongue falls out. Although, don't you think drooling down your jacket is a very attractive look? When men sleep, they tend to hold their willies. There's a very good reason why men keep their willies while sleeping. It dates back to the dawn of time, when cavemen needed to protect themselves and future generations from roaming testicle-eating wolves. However, female passengers nearby exclaim, 'Look at that! Typical! He can't take his hands off it!' Women are obsessed with penis envy. Women would never leave the house if they had penises. We should trade parts for a while. The streets would be completely empty. Flying is not a Rambling Man's natural state, but it is another way to get somewhere. You'll have to fly if you want to visit India or perform in Canada. Aeroplanes are unlikely to be a Rambling Man's preferred mode of air transportation; instead, I believe an airship is more likely. I'm fascinated by them, despite the fact that I've never seen one; they had ballrooms and everything. Years ago, Ian MacKintosh, the banjo player, sent me a wonderful postcard. It showed people in a German street pointing at a zeppelin in the sky. 'Taxi!' Ian had written on a balloon coming out of a guy's mouth. Nonetheless, commercial planes provide the Rambling Man with new opportunities for adventures. He can now travel far greater distances and visit exotic parts of the world that he could only read about previously. I first flew overseas while working as a welder in the shipyards. A fellow welder had mentioned how much he enjoyed his time in the Territorial Army (now known as the Army Reserve). He said he had a great time, and that he sometimes got a few weeks off work to go on exercises abroad. 'I could use some of that,' I reasoned. The whole concept appealed to my Rambling Man sensibilities, so I joined the parachute regiment. We practised on weekends, and I discovered that I liked jumping out of towers, balloons, and eventually helicopters and planes. I never experienced a runway landing on my first seven flights because I always jumped out of the plane with my parachute. I was eligible to go on trips abroad once I qualified. Marching, shooting a rifle, sleeping outside, lighting fires, and eating canned food were all enjoyable activities. They reminded me of the camping trips I used to take as a teenager. Then came the big day: I was given three weeks off from welding to travel to Cyprus for more intensive military training. We took one of those big military planes where you sit against the walls, then parachuted out into the pitch-black night and landed in the fields below. We had to find our regiment and then march through the night to a camp base where we started playing games and having a good time. It was a lot of fun. Our plane was struck by lightning on the way back from Cyprus. But I would never have known because there was no loud noise, searing flash of light, or terrifying ball of flames that you'd expect to see if your plane was struck by lightning. There was just a small bang, like a door slamming. I wasn't sitting next to a window, but I was in the seat opposite the toilet door, so I couldn't see out anyway. I happened to be eating treacle pudding at the time the plane was struck by lightning. I'd grown fond of military food - things you can take with you, like biscuits that turn into porridge after you soak them. The treacle pudding was especially tasty, and it came in a tin with a twisty razorblade thingy to open it with. I'd just unsealed it when the plane dropped hundreds of feet. Whoosh! My treacle pudding exploded from the tin. I'd never before seen a pudding levitate. I shot out my arm and caught it in my fist as quickly as I could. When we lost pressure, the oxygen masks dropped from the ceiling, but I ate my pudding first, then licked my sticky fingers. You wouldn't want treacle pudding all over your oxygen mask, would you? The captain eventually announced that we'd been struck by lightning and that there was a large hole in the fuel tank, so we'd have to land in Malta to fix it. I didn't mind. Another day off from the shipyards was ideal. In any case, the only barber shave I've ever had was in Malta. I enjoy being shaved with a sharp razor. It is one of the most luxurious things a man can do. And it was a godsend at the time because I had spots. Trying to shave around my acne was a nightmare for me.

During one of my tours of New Zealand, I went to an Auckland museum and saw a replica of the plane built by Richard Pearse, the first man to fly - he did it before the Americans. He did get airborne, but on his first flight, he crashed into a hedge on his farm. I used to fly in a biplane not much larger than his. It happened while filming for an Australian television show. I was in the front of this tiny two-seater plane, and the pilot, Bob, got in the back, which gave me a heart attack. 'Oh shit, how's he going to drive it?' I was thinking. I was quite nervous. 'Do we have parachutes on board?' I inquired of Bob. 'No,' he said. We're going to return.' I despise it when those in charge of your safety believe they are comedians. I attempted to strike up a friendly conversation. 'Have you ever parachuted from a plane?' I inquired. 'No,' he said. 'I can't think of a good reason to abandon a perfectly serviceable plane,' says the pilot. Then he bombarded me with questions about how I became a stand-up comedian. 'Eyes on the road, Bob,' I wanted to say, but instead I told him I was a funny folk singer who eventually graduated to doing solo concerts. 'That's the pinnacle for comedians,' I said, 'like flying solo is for you guys - only slightly more frightening.' Than, just to prove how terrifying he is, he began to loop the loop. Oh my god. My stomach was fine, but my arsehole pulsated. 'The first time I went solo, I chundered everywhere,' Bob said. I squeaked out, 'Me too.' After we landed, he told me that the camera battery had died while we were up there and that I should go back up to loop the loop. 'Are you kidding me?'

There are times when I wish people didn't know anything about me before meeting me, but that doesn't happen very often. They usually have an opinion of me, but I never know what it is because it depends on whether they've seen me perform or simply read slanderous things about me in the newspaper. I don't read newspaper articles about myself, so I'm not sure what strangers think I'm like - a funny man, a crazy beast, or the devil incarnate. Anyway, I once read an article that began, "Connolly's technique is extraordinary." I decided to read the rest of the book because I had no idea what my 'technique' was. 'Perhaps I can find out.' The article went on to say, 'He leaves the subject for hours on end and returns unerringly to where he left off.' That was nonsense. I never return to the same location; in fact, 'quite near' suffices for me, which is why I never became an airline pilot. What do I mean? There'd be a news report saying, 'The plane landed quite near Heathrow'... 'Bump! Bump! Bump! Bumpity Bump!'This is Captain Connolly, your pilot. We landed close to the airport. Everyone get out! There you have it... What are you upset about? Isn't this London? Okay, Londonish...

Fuck off with your luggage and family. Out! How can I leave on a ploughed field with you all sitting there? 'You're on your way.'

When you fly as much as I do, you're bound to encounter the occasional glitchy-poo. I had planned to meet Pamela in California. We were going to watch the royal wedding on TV together because Prince Charles and Diana were getting married. It was, after all, before Netflix. However, shortly after leaving Hong Kong, one of the engines failed catastrophically. I'm not sure what was wrong, but the plane was banking dangerously and ejecting fuel as it attempted to land. The majority of the passengers were terrified, but there was one man in front of me who was completely calm. 'It's nothing!' he exclaimed. I've crashed six times, so you're perfectly safe!' In Vietnam, he was a helicopter pilot. The pilot then announced, 'We're going to land in Tokyo.' When we landed, there were fire engines all along the runway, but nothing bad had happened, and everyone was relieved to have made it. The pilot then presented the passengers with a perplexing choice. 'You can fly in the same plane to Los Angeles, or we can get you a new plane, but it will take a long time to get another aircraft here and set it up,' he said. The old one is ready to go... but the decision is yours!' Waiting for a well-serviced, mechanically sound aircraft - even if it made you late - seems like a no-brainer to me. But the pilot had extraordinary persuasive skills, because at the end, everyone just shrugged and we took off in the same plane. But we didn't do it sober. We crammed everyone into First Class and had a wild party. People were insane, inebriated, and out of control. I believe the drinks were complimentary. There was a guy running around shagging everyone. He wore a sticker that read, 'I may be old, but I still get hot!' I don't believe there was a 'No Fly' list back then. I was flying from Canada to Los Angeles another time. We'd just gotten settled after taking off when a man jumped out of his seat and exclaimed, 'We're all going to die!' We're all going to die!' He insisted that we land. 'We're all going to DIE!!!' People were puking, and the staff was making their way down the aisle looking for a doctor to treat him. However, the only 'doctor' on board was an American actor who starred in a medical TV show. 'I'll give it a shot,' he said. He was extremely cool. 'Sit down, man,' he said from his seat. Everyone turned around to see who he was. He had a deep, authoritative voice that, surprisingly, worked. It was all over when the terrified man sat down. The right words said in the right way at the right time can make all the difference. On a flight from Glasgow to London, a man approached me. He introduced himself as the son of Pastor Jack Glass, a man who had plagued me for years by blaspheming me, protesting outside my concerts, and even throwing missiles at me. His son had clearly taken up his father's case. 'How would you feel if it was Judgment Day and God was judging you right now?' he asked. We had only just taken off. 'Fuck it!' I made a suggestion. 'My God - is that what you have to put up with?' said the guy next to me. But by then, Glass's son had fucked off. Yes, it is advantageous to be direct. Aside from the odd uncomfortable moment, I've had many wonderful flights, such as flying up to Galway, Ireland, to see where my family originated. For centuries, the sea has pounded that region. When I looked down, I saw all the huge stones - nature's Lego - just lying around. It was close to where John Alcock and Glaswegian Arthur Whitten Brown crashed after completing the first nonstop transatlantic flight. When Alcock was a prisoner of war during World War One, he dreamed up the trip while serving in the Royal Naval Air Service. In June 1919, he and Brown took off from Newfoundland in a twin-engine biplane. They made it across France to Ireland, but due to ice, hail, dense fog, and a failed engine, they were forced to crash-land in a bog in Connemara. Buggers, you're brave. As previously stated, if a Rambling Man had a favourite mode of transportation in the sky, it would most likely be an airship. I've always wanted to ride in one of those, but they stopped taking passengers after the Hindenburg disaster in 1937. I've heard they're making a comeback as 'greener' alternatives to aeroplanes. I believe there is a spy blimp in the sky near where I live, probably keeping an eye on Cuba or looking for drug runners from South America. It appears mysterious and shaky. I'm not a fan of anything that wobbles. I once had an encounter with a shaky UFO that gave me the scare of my life. I was playing my banjo on the deck of our Los Angeles home when I noticed something moving along the valley beneath me, weaving in and out of the buildings. I had no idea what it was. Then it turned and began to move towards me. I was paralyzed with fear when it turned to face me, looking like a strange airborne reptile. Was it a spaceship from another planet? My brain must have been doing the same thing that First Nations people did when they first saw European ships appear on their horizons. It finally dawned on me that it was a massive cluster of helium balloons tied together. They were affixed to an archway at the entrance to the used car dealership on Ventura Boulevard in the valley below. They'd been placed there to attract customers, but local pranksters had released them and they'd floated away. Everyone had a good time except for me. Jessie, the big one. I enjoy riding in helicopters. They're beautiful. Much more secure than their reputation. In a helicopter, I flew over New Zealand's stunning Fiordland region. It was Grizzly Adams country. Beautiful. If I were tortured with cigarette burns, I might admit it's better than Loch Lomond. They have fat turkey-like birds there, and they artificially rear them without their mothers using glove puppets. They even demonstrated how they perform a Punch and Judy show with ferrets and weasels to teach the birds about predators. Do you think I've seen everything?

I've also jumped out of a helicopter. You spring up from a seated position, your legs dangling outside. The guy in charge approaches and touches your shoulder, signalling that it's your turn to jump. Life in a helicopter is very different from life in an aeroplane. More at ease. You'll be flying over, say, Wellington when the pilot says, 'Fancy a coffee?' 'Yeah.' He'll land behind a coffee shop, and you'll get your macchiato before climbing back into the helicopter and taking off again. You come down and hide behind a tree if you need to pee. My worst 'needing to pee' experience was in Mogadishu, Somalia, while filming for Comic Relief. My first task upon arrival was to appear in front of the local power brokers and explain what we were doing. I was itching to pee in the tiny plane, but they only had those tiny narrow-neck bottles, and I'd have been pissed all over my legs. I just had to hold on until we touched down, but my back teeth were floating. I took off like a rocket the moment we touched down. The director of the Comic Relief show said it was the funniest thing he'd ever seen: three rows of dignitaries waiting to greet us on the tarmac, and me crashing right past them holding my willy. We didn't dare to film it, so it's a good thing they all laughed.

In Mogadishu, kids on their way to school say, 'Good morning!' And you respond with 'Good morning!' before they ask, 'How are you?' and burst out laughing. They are lovely children. They might let you play football with them if you can get the ball off them - which is difficult because they're very good. They are skilled at tricks such as bouncing the ball up and down and catching it on their heads.

Wonderful people. I once left my trike in Sydney and flew to Coober Pedy when I was in Australia. This was a wise decision. If you travel by road, you'll see a sign that says: 'Next Service 257 Miles'. Screw that. I also flew to Alice Springs, which has a nice appearance. We had dinner at a Swiss-Indian restaurant. It was fantastic - in the morning, we couldn't decide whether to fart or yodel. And we flew over Ayers Rock, as it was known back then before it was renamed Uluru, which seemed to be the end of the world. You suddenly have some perspective on prehistoric things. We're just a blip in the timeline compared to this. Coober Pedy, located halfway between Adelaide and Alice Springs, is the world's opal capital. I've never felt so hot in my entire life. The residents have dug their homes underground. Some are made of solid rock and have a very cool interior temperature. They even had an underground community swimming pool that had to be heated. My hotel in Coober Pedy was underground, which takes some getting used to. I turned out the light one night and couldn't find the bed. I'd never experienced such Stygian darkness before. It became quite frightening. It took a very long time to find my bed. Or even to locate a wall. I simply had to keep edging around until I came to a wall, then walk around the wall until I came to my bed. Coober Pedy truly resembles Australia. I had a strong desire to perform 'Waltzing Matilda'. The golf course there is not at all green. It's a sandy colour. To tee off, you carry a small square of AstroTurf with you around the course. And you don't have to worry about getting stuck in the sand because you're always in the sand. To be honest, I've never understood golf or golfers. I believe the Scots invented the game as a joke many years ago. 'Eh, Jimmy... hit this wee feather ball with this stick.' 'Are you joking, or what?' It wasn't meant to be taken seriously. And there was no rule against V-neck pullovers with wee lions and matching tartan trousers. Golfers deserve to be fucked and burned. Give the homeless golf courses. Planes are undeniably necessary for some trips, but if you only travel by plane, you may be deprived of the opportunity to truly experience places. I was in a bar in Invercargill, New Zealand's southernmost city, and a Scottish woman was serving drinks. 'This is a fantastic place,' she said. And I replied, 'Yeah? 'What do you mean, New Zealand?' 'Invercargill,' she said. It's a fantastic location. And I've travelled the globe.' 'Where have you been?' I inquired. She went through each location one by one. 'I've been to Dubai, Singapore,

Sydney, Melbourne, and up in Auckland!' It wasn't until later that I realised that was where the plane had landed on its way to Invercargill. She hadn't been anywhere in particular. But then people ask me, 'Have you ever been to Istanbul?' and I immediately say, 'Yes!' but then I realised I haven't seen the city. I just spent hours on a layover wandering around that massive airport looking for my fucking gate. Pamela careened recklessly towards me on one of those carry-on suitcases that transform into scooters, just as I thought I was on the right track. She'd bought it at an airport shop after injuring her knee and being unable to walk, but she had no idea how the brakes worked. She posed a serious threat to everyone in her path, and I had to run after her; that was MY Istanbul. During the performance, I told the Invercargill audience about an ugly mob running down the main street, with others joining them from side streets, chasing one poor guy. 'Come back!' they exclaimed. 'Do you consider yourself a Kiwi? 'You fucking traitor.' So I inquired, 'What's the story here?' 'Oh, it's that guy who hasn't seen The Lord of the Rings!' I admitted I was afraid to admit I hadn't seen it either. 'To be perfectly honest, I like movies with people in them!' I said. But that was before I played Dain II Ironfoot, King of the Dwarves, in The Hobbit: The Battle of the Five Armies. I loved the whole concept after appearing in that movie... even though I still haven't read Tolkien. I'm far too busy for people like him. I'm completely immersed in Proust and Dostoyevsky.

CHAPTER 4
WHAT DO STETSONS AND HAEMORRHOIDS HAVE IN COMMON?

I ADORE TRAMS. They travel at a reasonable speed, allowing you to see the world pass by gently rather than whooshing by too quickly. When I was a kid, my father would take me on the Glasgow 'caurs,' as they were known, to the city centre, where we would go to the Barras Sunday market. They made a lovely clankity clankity clank sound and smelled like metal and hot rubber. The conductors were fantastic, especially the female ones. They were witty and sassy. Everyone on the trams laughed as they told riddles and jokes. However, the Glasgow trams vanished in the early 1960s. People complained that the trams were clogging the roads and making traffic worse, so they were replaced by trolleybuses and, eventually, diesel buses. On the buses, the female employees continued their banter. 'I'd like a single to Drumchapel, please,' a guy would say. 'We're not going to Drumchapel!' said the conductress.But the front says "Drumchapel"!' 'Well, it says "India" on the tires, but we're not going there...!' she'd say with an old-fashioned look. Following the decommissioning of the Glasgow trams, some of them were imported into foreign cities. When Pamela and I visited Hong Kong in the 1980s, it was exciting to see the same trams that I'd known as a boy in Glasgow running around the island. They were renamed 'ding dings' after being dressed up in primary colours with advertisements for Fuji and Mitsubishi. Melbourne has the world's largest urban tram network. Someone approached me on a Melbourne tram once and asked for my autograph. Soon after, another curious person approached and asked, 'Excuse me... are you a film star?' 'Nope, I'm not a movie star... and I don't think I ever will be!' I replied. What was I thinking? I never expected to make fifty films. Melbourne holds a special place in my heart, and I adore the Australian wry sense of humour. Melbourne is regarded as the epicentre of gunzeldom. A gunzel is similar to a trainspotter in that they know a lot about things that no one cares about. You'll be taking a photograph somewhere when you hear someone ask, 'Is that a B13 you've got there?'

'What?'

'It's your camera.'

'I'm not sure.'

'I believe you'll find B13 if you open the door and look under the hinge.'

'Oh fuck, it does.'

'That's what I assumed. It is identical to a B15. It was changed in 1964. The hinge on the B15 is slightly longer, and the door is slightly narrower. They discovered that shortening the hinge and widening the door allowed for much easier access. It was designed by Thompson. 'He died in 1974.'

You're beginning to back away. 'Is that correct?'

'Aye. I have the B17, which has a longer door and a slightly different switch inside that transfers gunzel power to the ignition switch...'

They are obsessed. You have to be blunt and cut them off if you don't want to stand there for another hour. 'Pardon me... 'Will you fuck off?'

Trains are just as appealing as trams. I once produced a television show called Tracks Across America in which I travelled through Minnesota, North Dakota, and Montana. It was a fantastic journey. The only issue is the 'woo hoo' noise, which they make all night. The train driver sits in the front and does it at each crossing. The phrase 'whoo hooo hooo' is overused. But you get used to it after a while. Your mind appears to simply tune it out. Taking a shower on the train is difficult, but I discovered that some people get very creative with it. The guard on my train reported seeing three guys showering together. 'I won't tell you what they were doing, but one of them was upside down,' he said. Do you think his athletics are impressive? I'm not sure what a guard was doing walking in on three adults taking a private shower, but there was apparently a noise complaint... "Whooo Hooo?"

The shower has a seat, but it's the toilet. You can sit on it while showering and it will help you stay balanced. Otherwise, you'll be jolted back and forth every time the train lurches. That should help you soap yourself, but it's also a heartbreaker. It's actually a very efficient shower. The temperature is ideal. You have to pry yourself out of the bathroom cubicle to get your towel, but it's next to your sleeping compartment, so no one should see your bare arse. Every aspect of a moving train has the potential for comedy. It's entertaining to watch people try to maintain their balance. They walk in an unusual manner. They walk up the train, and you both laugh as they squeeze past you. Make a brief remark. They are thrown sideways onto objects and end up in people's laps. It's a lot of fun. The trip took about three weeks and was accompanied by a crew of about six people. The beds were wide enough for two people and folded down from the wall - these are known as Murphy beds. There was a restaurant car that rotated through the station. Because they couldn't fit everyone in at once, they gave you times when you could go for dinner. It was delicious food. I used to enjoy the bean roll and ate it almost every night. It sounds disgusting, but it was delicious. We'd drive overnight to the next state, then get up and start filming.

My favourite state along the train route was Montana. The people there were cowboys . . . and Native Americans. And the occasional yodeller. I met a true yodeller in a town called Shelby. He stood playing his guitar for me next to the railroad tracks, and when he started singing I could barely believe my ears – it was amazing, a real joy to listen to. He called it 'fancy cowboy yodelling', something he learned from his father when he was a boy. He told me his father would yodel old cowboy songs whenever he was happy. As he started to play another tune, I heard a 'woo hoo' in the distance, and a train flew past us as we sang together:

All around the water tanks,
waiting for a train
A thousand miles away from home,
sleeping in the rain
I walked up to a brakeman,
to give him a line of talk
He says 'If you've got money,
I'll see that you don't walk.'

Many of the people I met in Montana were ranchers and farm workers. Some were rovers who travelled from farm to farm, true Rambling Men. Workers who put in the effort. It's a hard life, but it's also simple in many ways. I went to a radio station where there was an entire program dedicated to exchanging items. People swapped farm machinery and other items I'd never heard of, such as a 'gizmo' for a 'gecko'. It was a rather dull program, but it gave me some ideas. It would be a great way to get rid of my floral Hawaiian shirts if Florida had a swap station. I'm tired of them. I'd also trade my wife for a Winnebago. I'd love to own a Winnebago. I've always thought it would be a great way to live, pulling into lay-bys and sleeping for the night, then meeting new people and living your life in true Rambling Man style. Unfortunately, I don't think you can do it any longer - people with parking lots won't let you stay the night.

I met some real hobos on that train ride. I don't care if the word "hobo" is no longer politically correct. It's simply another name for a Ramblin Man... or perhaps a subset of Rambling Men. In any case, the term is commonly used. Look at any high fashion website today and you'll notice that having expensive, unstructured, designer 'hobo bags' is in. They're inspired by the carryalls used by men and women seeking work across America during the Great Depression. I've been carrying that type of casual shoulder bag for at least fifty years, so I must be a truly fashion-forward Rambling Man, don't you think?

In any case, there are far more derogatory terms for travellers than "hobo," including "derelict," "bum," "vagrant," and "beggar." What is the distinction between a hobo, a tramp, and a bum? Some define a 'hobo' as a migratory person who wants to work, a tramp as someone who will work if necessary, and a bum as someone who does not want to work at all. Some believe the term "hobo" is an abbreviation for "Homeward Bound," which referred to soldiers returning home after the American Civil War ended. Others claim that the term derives from 'home-boys,' referring to farmhands who travelled around with hoes and other tools. However, regardless of terminology, a common theme in the history of these Rambling Men subsections is that they traversed the country on boxcars, which are train carts. Trains and Rambling Men are inextricably linked, as you can see.

Martin Scorsese directed Boxcar Bertha, a film about a famous hobo loosely based on Bertha Thompson's autobiography. She was used to jumping freight trains. Boxcar Bertha is a fantastic name! In the USA there are many famous hobos with wonderful names, such as: 'Frog', 'Hobo Lump', 'Connecticut Tootsie', 'Grain Car George' and 'Angie Dirty Feet'. There was also Boxcar Willie, a musician who sang songs like "The Lord Made a Hobo Out of Me" and "Hobo Heaven."

A hobo's dreams are like angel wings, carrying him wherever he wants to go.

Jimmy Logan, a classmate of mine, became a nomad in South Africa. He was an intriguing individual. People constantly told him what he could have been. He was amusing and could have made a good comedian. He was a good football player who went to South Africa to play for the Bloemfontein Rangers, but he never returned home. I ran into him because his brother asked me to look for him while I was touring there, and I did. 'Jimmy, what happened?' I inquired. 'We were getting fifty pounds a week, and wine was fifty pence a bottle,' he explained. I didn't want to return. 'I was overjoyed.' He simply took the trains from town to town. He was on the front page of the Glasgow newspapers when he died. 'I'm a hobo, and Billy Connolly gave me a hundred pounds,' he said.

I met another modern hobo, a lovely musician, while filming Tracks Across America. He was an excellent guitarist and singer. He travelled around the country playing music and working on ranches, then sending money home to his wife. What I liked best about him was his apparent happiness. He told me that there were between one and two hundred hobos on the train at any given time. However, he also stated that things had changed in the hobo world since 9/11, and that it was becoming increasingly difficult to board a train and get inside a car.

And I heard there's a punk sect that occasionally travels by train. A punk hobo subculture! They appear to be a nightmare to encounter. Violent. There have been some heinous hobo murders. It's all very Clockwork Orange. When there is an increase in the number of unemployed people and economic hardship in certain areas of the United States, hobo numbers - and competition for a seat on a train - increase. I wished I could join them because I still have a romantic notion of train-hopping, even though it would be difficult at my age and in my state of health. But the hobos weren't drinking free margaritas in First Class. They were in the department of Sore Arse. Anyway, because of my Parkinson's disease, I shake so much that I can sit in my living room with my eyes closed and pretend I'm on a freight train.

Meeting Native Americans at county fairs and festivals is one of my favourite memories from filming the Across the Tracks series. I loved seeing them dance in their traditional attire, complete with all the gear. Wonderful. I enjoy the chants, but I've always wondered what the different sounds meant. When I asked if it was words or sounds, a tribesman replied, 'Just sounds.' 'It's like a mantra, but we know the sounds,' he explained. It's like a language, and we need to keep it alive.' He told me a story about two boys fishing from a tree that had fallen into the river. One sat at one end and the other at the other, but neither caught anything. A senior citizen passed by. 'Are you catching anything, boys?' he inquired. 'We're not getting any bites,' they said. 'I'm not surprised,' the elder said. You're not following orders.' He slung the line into the water, then yanked it back in a jerking, rhythmic motion while chanting, 'Heya, haya hi, heya heya...' He got a bite right away. He taught the boys that in order to be a successful fisherman, they must fish in the rhythm of the song.

It was incredible to see the tribespeople dancing and stamping their feet. 'Hey Yey yey yey yey yey yey yey yey Suede fringe, feathers, and beads are embellished. It was fantastic. We had arrived early at the festival site, but no one was there yet. So we hung out and ate hamburgers, thinking to ourselves, 'Oh, it's just another fair day in America.' Then we heard, 'Dumdododo Dumdodo Dumdodododododododododododododododododododododod They danced their way through the gate. 'Hey... eye eye,' I say. Brilliant. I was transported to the Western plains, where I sat on my horse with the 'Indians' surrounding me. I used to go to see 'Cowboy and Indian' movies as a kid, and the audience would cheer for the 'Indians' and boo for the cowboys, because Glaswegians identify with the underdog. The cowboys represented power. The 'Indians' also had better horses and fabulous jewellery, particularly Navaho. In New Mexico, I met the Navajo and the Hopi people. For years, I've been wearing a silver and turquoise Navajo bracelet.

I met a man who wore the most fantastic outfits when we stopped in El Paso, a lovely little town along the train route where lucha libre is very popular. He was an exótico, a type of Mexican wrestler who often fought in drag. Cassandro was dressed to the nines, with white and gold boots, a coiffed blond mullet, silver eyeshadow, and a long black and gold cape that he whipped off as he approached me, revealing a white and black bodysuit covered in diamanté. It was quite a sight. Cassandro explained that he'd been an exótico since 1987 and had faced a lot of discrimination as an openly gay wrestler. He was abused by women who mistook him for beating up their husbands or boyfriends, and he was once stabbed in the stomach by a woman wielding nail clippers. He told me that his father had been absent for most of his life, but that they'd finally been able to talk and become close again a few years ago, and that he now considered his father his best friend. That was wonderful to hear.

Rocketbuster is a fantastic boot store in El Paso. They make the best handmade custom cowboy boots in the world. The boots were designed around specific themes. I'd like to wear the 'Eddie Cochrane' boot on one foot and the 'Buddy Holly' boot on the other, but you'd have to get both pairs. I already own some of their boots, which are my favourites. My favourite boots are the 'Devil With The Blue Dress On'. They were featured in a Canadian magazine called Cowboys and Indians, which was all about jewellery and clothing. I called Rocketbuster and they said, 'Send a template of your feet.' They sent me fantastic boots - black with white stitching, with red flames and skeletons in blue sombreros drinking tequila from bottles, and female devils in blue miniskirts with red hair and sunglasses, playing blue and red maracas. They were even better than I had hoped. And they fit perfectly. Pamela got me some nice Rocketbuster boots. My own foot tattoos are replicated on them. However, you must be careful not to overdo the cowboy look. What did Keith Richards say to me about the Stetson? "What do Stetsons and haemorrhoids have in common?" Every arsehole gets one eventually.'

CHAPTER 5
THE HAPPY WANDERER

A MAN WALKED UP AND DOWN THE Aisles AT ONE OF MY CONCERTS IN SCOTLAND. 'I know you think this man is going for a pee, but he's a hiker, a rambler,' I told the audience. This man deserves to be recognized. This is in fact a public right of way. He does this every fifteen minutes to ensure that it remains open for you and me. I believe we should give him a standing ovation. He and his kind have gone unnoticed for far too long. He's been keeping the highways and byways clear of vagrants, thieves, and fucking perverts... In fact, I believe we should all sing a verse of "The Happy Wanderer" to him. Then I sang, 'Oh I love to go a-wandering, Along the mountain track,' and the entire audience sang along with the chorus: 'Fallderee fallderah...'

That kind of thing makes me happy. That's when it transforms into a concert, a true one-off. Every night, there won't be a guy wandering around. When that happens, the audience knows they're watching a comedian who isn't just a joke-teller, who doesn't just show up with a bunch of jokes. A true Rambling Man recognizes the need to think on his feet. Things will not always be rosy. You may be without a place to sleep; plans you thought you'd made may fall through, leaving you with nowhere to stay and forcing you to sleep on the street. I recall having to sleep under a bridge in Aberfoyle, near Loch Lomond. There were three arches on this bridge. I fell asleep under the middle one, but when I awoke a few hours later, the water had risen and my legs were submerged. I had to get my arse moving. I walked down the street and saw some empty, half-finished houses, so I went inside and slept in the rafters. I was balanced between two planks, so God knows what kept me up because I was only lying on plaster. By all rights, I should have collapsed into the room. However, I did not. I slept soundly. I did a lot of stuff like that, just using whatever I could find - shop doorways, empty sheds... It was usually satisfactory. People were different back then; they didn't seem to mind - in fact, they seemed to enjoy it. Hitchhiking was commonplace, and most people who picked you up were courteous. That was my experience, at least. 'What are your plans?' 'What are you planning to do there?' Oh, la la. It was beautiful. They enjoyed hitchhiking and thought it was a great way to get around. People would give me food as well as records and other items they thought I might enjoy. See, I was always carrying an instrument. That was a clear indication that I was on my way to a gig. They would occasionally put me up for the night. 'Come on... you're welcome to stay at my house!' The 1960s were remarkable. Then we started hearing about people being attacked on the road. It's a disgrace. But there was a lovely atmosphere, a joyful feeling before that. It was all new in the 1960s. There was a spirit of adventure and optimism. Because there was a disregard for convention and responsibilities, it was the ideal decade for Rambling Men.

Homelessness was viewed in a different light back then. Homeless people have existed throughout history, but they are not the same as wandering folk. You can be a Rambling Man without a permanent address or a home, so you're technically homeless, but not everyone who is homeless is a Rambling Man. Again, it all comes down to your mindset and outlook on life. And hitchhikers may be considered homeless - at least for the duration of their journey, which could be years. Hitchhiking is an important part of the Rambling Man's travels - or it was until they started passing laws against it and motorists began to think it was a risky business. There are a few states in America, for example, that have made hitchhiking illegal, but many people still do it. It's ingrained in their history and culture. During the Vietnam War, a driver with a full car would tap the roof of their car to indicate that there wasn't enough room for a soldier who wanted to hitch a ride. I've been fortunate enough to find space in hundreds of strangers' cars and have spent many enjoyable hours chatting and enjoying the free ride. I used to go on vacation by myself, hitchhiking with my banjo, and I loved it. Meeting new people and playing music with them on the road. I'd occasionally spend the night in train stations, sleeping on a bench in the waiting room. I tied a fishing line between my ankle and my banjo in case it was stolen. I remember sleeping in a freezing waiting room somewhere, but the heater only stayed on for a few minutes and I had to get up all night to turn it back on. I wanted to go to France when I was about nineteen and on vacation from the shipyards. I hitchhiked from Hamilton, Scotland, to Dover, and then took the ferry to Calais. I had Catch-22 by Joseph Heller in my pocket and was eager to read it. On the boat, I read it before falling asleep on the cabin floor. The crew, who were returning to England, woke me up. I stepped off the ferry, but I was alone and had nowhere to go. I started itching again, this time to Dunkirk, where my cousin and some Glasgow guys were staying. I was picked up by one man and sat in the back of his car with his daughter. We were all laughing so hard that I was tickling her to make her laugh, and he was laughing as well. He pulled over to get some ice cream, and he even got one for me. So there I was, sitting in the back with the man's daughter, eating ice cream. It was fantastic.

When I arrived in Dunkirk, I walked through the town to the youth hostel on the coast, where I met my cousin John, a Rambling Man. He wasn't working, so he was just hanging out in Dunkirk. He'd arrived at the youth hostel and liked the people there, so he decided to stay for a while. I had planned to visit Amsterdam but never got there. I just hung out with John and played music. I didn't have a banjo, but I did have an old guitar tuned to sound like one. People used to give us money when we played in the street. In Dunkirk, I met a lovely woman named Suzette. She was about eighteen years old and round and curvy. She had dark-brown curly hair and large cheeks. She was eating liver she had prepared herself in the hostel, which smelled delicious. I was starving and sitting there staring at her. She looked up and noticed that I was staring at her. I said, 'Bonjour.' 'Bonjour, monsieur.' she said. 'Would you like to go for a walk?' I asked. Promenade?' When she said, 'Oui,' we went for a walk, and I wished I could speak French. When we saw a sailing boat, I exclaimed, 'Bateau!' 'Oui, bateau.' she said. We continued walking until we came across a fishing boat. 'Poisson bateau,' I said, and she said, 'Oui. 'Boat Poisson.' She must have grown tired of my conversational style. We entered a café and saw a glass case with cakes inside. Because one of them was shaped like a fishing boat, I called it 'poisson bateau gateau.' She erupted in laughter. She purchased liver and onions for me. Delicious. She reminds me of liver whenever I think of her now. The 1960s were a great era to be alive. Hitchhiking allows you to skip ahead to your destination, but in order to explore a place, you must take your time. Manhattan is my favourite city to walk around in. There's always something new to discover there. On the streets of New York, selling pretzels and hot dogs, you meet wonderful people. One vendor I always saw selling small kites, and another sold toy birds that chirped when you put water in them. 'Bring your birds here!' I once passed him while dressed in a vintage bowling jacket with the name 'Buster' embroidered on the front. 'Everybody knows your name now, Buster!' he yelled after me. There is only one rule for walking in the city: you must know where to pee. What is my solution? You stingy bastard, if you need to pee, buy a coffee. I used to walk to Mannys' music store on 45th Street and 7th Avenue. It sold new and used instruments and was brightly coloured on the inside. On Broadway, there was another music store I liked that sold sheet music, instruction books, and records. I also enjoyed going to the Bottom Line, a small music venue where you could see live performances by various musicians. It's no longer standing, but it was a legendary Greenwich Village club located between Mercer and Greene Streets. I once saw Loudon Wainwright there. I played it about twenty years ago, and Keith Richards came to see me. I enjoyed strolling around Union Square, which was close to where I used to live. I liked going to The Coffee Shop for tea and then going to Barnes and Noble to browse. I also saw Loudon live in Barnes and Noble, where he was performing a small concert and promoting a book. I saw John Prine in New York once and fell in love with him. He was a pleasant companion. Covid is a fucking jerk. It took a lot of brilliant people. I enjoy meeting true New Yorkers - people who were born and raised in the city. They are reminiscent of Glaswegians. They're amusing and tell it like it is. Nothing is sugar-coated for them. Archie, a Glaswegian friend of mine, was working on a ship docked in New York and decided to go for a walk. He approached a couple of police officers who were standing on a corner twirling their sticks like they used to. 'Excuse me... could you tell me the location of the Empire State Building?' 'You got a dollar?' said one of the cops. 'Yeah,' Archie replied, reaching into his pocket. 'Then buy a fucking map!' said the cop. When I lived in New York, the cops were always courteous. 'Good day, Connolly!' They didn't want you to stop and talk to them; all they wanted was for you to shout your name. Recognize that they are aware of your identity. Edinburgh is another fantastic city for a stroll. The entire city is built clinging to the face of an extremely steep hill, and the city streets are steeped in history. However, the cobblestones are prone to tripping. When people trip on the street, they may pretend to see someone they recognize. That makes me happy. That kind of thing always made me laugh, and it seemed to make others laugh as well. It exemplifies something I've heard about comedy: the ever-present threat of inanimate objects. I suppose it applies to slapstick at the very least. The Three Stooges, Charlie Chaplin, Harold Lloyd, Laurel and Hardy, and others were known for their rough-and-tumble acts. They used to scream at me. I see modern versions on American television in shows like America's Funniest Home Videos, which are just clips of people getting into mishaps. They're very popular, but they can come across as fake or cruel at times. When you're in Edinburgh, you can tell the time in a spectacular way. Is it exactly one o'clock? Boom. Castle with a cannon. I once went to get a Tattoo. This perplexes visitors from other countries. 'How are you able to "get a tattoo"? 'Don't you "go get one?"' What I enjoy most about the annual Royal Edinburgh Military Tattoo on the esplanade of Edinburgh Castle is watching the guys dance Scottish reels together - all those kilts swinging at the same time. 'But what about Billy?' I hear you inquire. 'How come it's called a Tattoo?' I'll be damned if I know. Someone said it sounded like tapping because they used to tattoo you by tapping two sticks together in a drumming rhythm. I just looked it up, and it had something to do with pubs closing early so soldiers could get some shut-eye. Why have people throughout history attempted to prevent men from having fun? My friend told me that for Christmas, he gave his wife a large glass of whisky. She spit out her first sip. 'How are you drinking that?' 'See?' he replied. You think I'm out having fun every night?'

I used to walk to and from my gigs at Edinburgh's Usher Hall. It's a fine old hall, fit for the grand city of Edinburgh, with its wide, open spaces and breathtaking views. There's plenty of live music, poetry, and theatre in town. The Edinburgh Fringe Festival is the best comedy festival on the planet, or at least the best I've ever seen. It has a lovely rough edge to it, with an egalitarian mix of amateurs and emerging professionals. Previously, the well-known Traverse Theatre would host a Fringe promotional event. The Traverse had a small courtyard where you could bring your poster and sing a few songs from your show, and people could decide whether or not they wanted to see it. I was performing in The Welly Boot Show, which I co-wrote. We were waiting in line to perform our two songs, and there were a couple of miners ahead of us, followed by Yehudi Menuhin. He was hiding his violin beneath his jacket because it was raining and he wanted to keep it dry. I liked how he was in line with everyone else. He went forward after the miners and did his part, and, predictably, he brought the house down. 'Yeah, I like this,' I thought. This is how things should be.'

Walking through the countryside allows you to be part of nature, in the middle of the landscape of wheat fields, birds, and animals, feeling the wind and smelling the road rather than just watching it whizz by. Northern Ireland is an excellent location for this. It's wonderful to get lost in the countryside there. There are also fairy trees. A lone hawthorn tree growing in the middle of a field is a magical gateway or portal between our world and the world of fairies in Celtic folklore. These trees are sometimes surrounded by a circle of stones. Farmers never cut them down and will go to great lengths to avoid them in case the fairies become enraged. Local lore is very important to the people there. I'm not going to say it's garbage because it appeals to me. Roads have had to be rerouted in the past to avoid the fairy thorns,and building plans have had to be altered. It's bad luck if you damage one. There was one in a quarry in Fermanagh that they refused to move. But they eventually did, and shortly afterwards, there was an explosion that killed three people. What else can I say?

Many people I know believe in fairies. In Ireland, this is a deeply held belief. They are not the fairies from children's books who live among the dandelions. They are people from another dimension who came to live among us thousands of years ago and are still here. They live in tunnels and warrens, but they are not small people; they are of average size. They appear on various occasions to participate in human celebrations, funerals, and life in general. They live their lives alongside the people. We can't see them because they're invisible, though people have reported seeing them out of the corner of their eyes. Fairy belief does not coexist with Catholicism, but many Catholics secretly believe it and keep it to themselves. The trees in which they live are miraculously clean and tidy, but when branches fall close to the tree, they are left there because that is the closest people will go. They take everything very seriously, and they don't take jokes about it well, because there's nothing to laugh about. They'll tell you stories about people who were told they couldn't open a supermarket because it was in fairy land, but they did it anyway... and they lost all their money. They interpret this as proof of the fairies' power. I was familiar with a fairy tree near the border between Northern Ireland and Ireland. You knew it the moment you saw it. Wild and lovely. 'Good morning, fairies!' you must say as you pass by. Walking can be exhausting. I went to Caithness, near John O'Groats, where waterfalls go up instead of down. It's an extraordinary place. You get the best aerobic exercise there. There are sheer cliffs that lead down to the sea. If you wanted to wash your clothes by the sea, as many people did, it's the ultimate aerobic exercise: a zillion steps up and down. Women would bring their baskets to pick up the catch caught by fishermen. They'd race back up, and the first one to the top got a free mackerel. Those ladies had steel buns.

I adore Scotland's northeast. It takes me back to my days of folk singing. We used to spend a lot of time playing John O'Groats and Wick. You changed trains in Inverness, and the world changed. The scenery is different. The terrain is harsh and hard, almost tundra-like. Wick can get extremely cold. When I was there, Malcolm, my sound man, would turn to me with his teeth chattering and say, 'Billy, remember when we were sitting on the beach in Dubai, roasting in the sun, and you said, "It won't be long until we're in Wick?"' That's just another example of the Scottish tendency to look at the sun and say, 'We'll pay for this!' The weather changes quickly in the north-east, which some see as a flaw, but I see as Scotland's best asset. The weather can change in five seconds. You don't know what to wear, and life is generally unpredictable. I just wish the weather forecasters on TV would tell it like it is: 'It's fucking pishing again. 'Watch yersel on the mountains: someone fell off, they're fucking slippery...'

It can be difficult to live in such harsh conditions up there. It gives people a unique personality. I've discovered that they are somewhat distant people who don't communicate easily. But, like all distant people, when they do decide to communicate with you, they are warm and welcoming. When you make a friend of the north-eastern people, it's for life. You'd have to have an operation to have them removed. Very good people to have on your side. I've spent many happy years there, playing and just wandering around. There are many ramblers in the Highlands. Ramblers are not the same as Rambling Men. They are people who go hiking along a predetermined route in order to see sights, caves, rivers, and so on... and then they return home. They go walking specifically to look for those kinds of things, whereas Rambling Men just leave without caring where they go or what they might find. Ramblers have the Rambling Man spirit, but they are more organised. They are dressed in anoraks. They're a bit... olive green. Except for the farmers, they like to think of themselves as being from the countryside. And the farmers are fiercely protective of their land. They don't like people walking through their fields. During my tours, it was always important to me to walk around town before my show. I'd fly, drive, or ride my bike to a town, but then I'd always go for a walk to see what kind of place it was. I'd see the people, look in the shop windows, see the town centre, the monuments - and talk to a few people. So, when I walked onstage, I'd have a good idea of who the audience was, what they liked, and what they found funny. I would have been lost without it, so walking was an important part of my act. Looking in store windows can reveal a lot about your target audience. I once did an interview in a Wellington boot store in Australia while browsing. 'A lot of people just dismiss the welly as an ordinary piece of rainwear - nonsense,' I told them, before picking up the various boots: 'Here's your worker's boot... the see-through flasher's welly... your liberal welly - the true blue.' And then I discovered the best of them all, the Scottish: 'Here you have a low-cut, tartan welly, great for Highland dancing, good sturdy see-through heel for the high kicks, with elastic gussets - say no more.'

I was one of the first people to walk across Sydney Harbour Bridge just for fun. Because the well isn't suitable for climbing, I wore my cowboy boots. Paul Hogan from Crocodile Dundee actually worked on the bridge, so he'll have walked across it. But, aside from the workers and builders, I was one of the first to walk over it. The bridge opened in 1932, and the premier of New South Wales was supposed to cut the ribbon. However, a random Irishman named Francis de Groot charged up on a horse with a sword and sliced the ribbon first. He was taken to a psychiatric hospital but was found to be sane. They charged him two pounds for the ribbon and four pounds for disturbing the peace. I adore the lunatic edge. I was doing concerts at the Sydney Opera House at the time I got to walk over the bridge, so I asked one of the guys who maintains the building, 'How can I see the Opera House from an angle people haven't seen before?' He said, 'You can walk on the roof.' So, that afternoon, I was up there, looking down from that incredible piece of architecture. I've always admired extraordinary feats of engineering around the world, such as the Eiffel Tower, the Gateway Arch in St. Louis, and the Seven Mile Bridge in the Florida Keys. Going across the Forth Bridge in Scotland is a special treat. Especially the old one, the Victorian one. The modern one was across from the Victorian one. I was filming there once and said, 'That modern one has one function: to stand upon and look at this.' I'm always impressed by engineering feats like that. 'Men put that together with tools,' I think. It honours the glory of working men. The things they've created. I enjoyed highlighting them in my television travel shows. I recall being on a loch in Scotland and showing the camera the man-made islands that conceal Glasgow's waterworks. They just look like islands with coniferous trees on them, and they're very pretty - you'd never guess they're functional. Every day, however, the structure within them pumps millions of gallons of fresh water into the city. I enjoy highlighting what humans are capable of. That's the proud welder in me. I used to take photographs of things I liked while walking around the world. During one of my world tours, I took a series of bizarre photos. I photographed the Sydney Harbour Bridge up close, just a few steel girders. When I was in New York, I took a picture of the Empire State Building from about eighteen inches away - it just looks like a piece of concrete. Later, in the Sahara Desert, I pointed my camera down at the sand. When I returned home with what I thought were very artistic World Tour photographs, I showed them to my father. He thought I was crazy. He didn't get the joke.I enjoy visiting art galleries and museums. I had special access to the Vatican in Rome because I was filming a BBC TV show called The Bigger Picture about Scottish art there. I walked around for days and saw fantastic art that had been hidden away from the main displays for centuries. In the first episode, I traced the journeys of many young Scottish artists to Rome in the eighteenth century. In the third episode, I even had my portrait painted by the famous Scottish artist John Bellany. I thought he might have given it to me, but he didn't. Bastard. When I'm out walking, I have to keep an eye out because I could be caught off guard. I was out one day in London when a man came up behind me. 'Billy! Billy! Could you please sign an autograph for my grandson, Gavin?' 'Sure.' A young boy approached us. On his scrap of paper, I wrote: To Gavin - Best Wishes, Billy Connolly. I started walking away when I heard: 'Billy!... Billy! 'I apologise once more for interrupting your walk,' he says. 'However, Gavin was hoping you could tell him to fuck off.' 'Sure,' I replied. 'Gavin? 'Fuck it!' 'YESSS!' exclaimed the youngster.

I did a lot of walking in Rotorua, New Zealand, and in Te Puia's Whakarewarewa Valley. It's known for its geothermal activity, so the lakes and bubbling mud pools look like they're ready to serve your porridge. The forests are ancient and beautiful for hiking, and the town is bright and welcoming. And they have an extremely virile geyser that has many daily ejaculations (some prefer the word "eruptions," but if you saw this thing, you'd agree with me). But the highlight of my New Zealand tour was walking along Ninety Mile Beach to where the Tasman Sea meets the Pacific Ocean in New Zealand's far north. Cape Reinga, or Te Rerenga Wairua - a Mori name for the spiritual pathway - is located at the tip of the Aupouri Peninsula. It's a very special and sacred location. The Mori believe that the spirit departs from there for the ancestral home - the end point of their earthly world. In a pub, two men were conversing.

'What would you do if we discovered we only had three minutes until the end of the world?'

'I would shag anything that moved. 'How would you react?'

'I'd remain motionless.'

CHAPTER 6
WITCHETTY GRUBS AND CULLEN SKINK

MOST WANDERING MEN When it comes to food, you can't afford to be too picky. When you're on the road, you eat whatever is available. Some of them can cook over an open fire, but even when I used to go camping, that was out of my league. That wasn't something I did much of. I did, however, cook potatoes. I'd wrap them in tinfoil and set them on fire. They were delectable. And if I caught a small fish, I'd cook it in foil as well. I've been living in Florida for several years, and people here enjoy cooking outside. Not me. I mean, I enjoy a good burnt sausage as much as the next guy, but I'd rather make a quick curry in my air-conditioned kitchen without having to compete with insects, birds, palm rats, and uninvited humans. To be sure, when I smell barbecued meat wafting over my neighbour's fence, I think to myself, 'Maybe I'm missing out on something great!' And the aroma of the sweet, spicy food that the Haitian family down the street cooks in their backyard makes me hungry. They sit around listening to music and eating, laughing and shouting... I really wish they'd invite me. In recent years, the men in our family have established a Christmas tradition of deep-frying a turkey - which, according to the news, is most definitely an outdoor activity, given the annual kitchen explosions and house fires. I grew up eating school dinners, so that's the type of food I prefer. Shepherd's pie, sponge and custard, mince and potatoes, sausages, apple pie and custard, and caramel pie and custard are all available. The only thing I didn't like were the disgusting vegetables that were served on the side of your plate. But I would have gone to the moon and back for more shepherd's pie. My macaroni and cheese is excellent, but I could live on curry every day. When I'm travelling, however, I try to be open to local cuisine and am rarely disappointed. What's the point of visiting exotic places if you're always looking for familiar things? If you only eat at home, you'll miss out on some of the world's best dishes, such as those found at Hong Kong's roadside food markets, yakitori bars in Japan, and Cuban food trucks in the Florida Keys. I enjoy American roadside food, though I wouldn't eat it all the time because it's not exactly good for your colon; however, it's perfect when you're on the road. Breakfast is best served in traditional American diners. My favourite dish is bacon and eggs with American biscuits and gravy. I adore how Americans prepare bacon; it's a very different cut from British bacon, which is wider at one end and usually has a lining of fat down one side. When cooked, American bacon is a narrow strip streaked with fat that becomes crispy. It's delectable. My fried eggs must be 'over easy'. It's wonderful to sit down to such a breakfast. If you're in the mood, home fries are delicious, but they fill you up quickly. It's excellent fortification if you're riding your motorcycle in the rain. However, I do not believe that American coffee complements breakfasts. Tea is far superior. It belongs to the same gang. Some greeting-faced Britons dislike the way Americans make tea. True, some fundamental errors are frequently made - a mug of lukewarm water with a wee teabag in a paper bag sitting beside it - but that's not going to change, so it's best to just shut up and get on with it. Some roadside diners in America specialise in unusual foods such as alligator jerky and roadkill. I enjoy trying such delicacies, but I believe that a small amount of them goes a long way. Wild dogs are tasty, but nothing beats a nice bit of rat in the morning... on second thought, just give me a hot dog with some fries. On Route 66, my typical lunch was a double hamburger with a cheeseburger and a cup of tea. We'd go to Chinese restaurants for dinner, and I'd order prawn fried rice with Chinese tea.

In Texas, I enjoyed chicken fried steak. It's steak fried in batter, like chicken, and it's delicious. And, like the locals, I drank soft drinks. I enjoyed the Mexican dish huevos rancheros for breakfast. Texas is ideal for this. I mistook huevos rancheros for Ranch Cheerios, but it's actually fried eggs with hot sauce. Tasty. I discovered it was a favourite of one of my heroes, Peter Cook. When I can get it, I enjoy good soul food. In Louisiana, I had crawfish pot pie, which was delicious. The crawfish was minced and tasted similar to prawns, but even better. Hank Williams sang about crawfish pie and the bayou. Oh my goodness, crawfish pie... Gumbo is a strong, thick soup made with shellfish or meat, celery, onions, and peppers that I enjoy as well. I like it best when there are whole shrimp in it. But my personal favourite has been Sweetie Pie's Restaurant in St Louis. Miss Robbie Montgomery, the proprietor, was a member of the Ikettes, the legendary backing singers for Ike and Tina Turner who would tear up the stage with their electric performances. 'Yeah, I used to shake my tail feathers,' she laughed, 'but now the tail feathers broke, and I can't shake it any longer - I've gotten too old for that!' She told me that when she was on tour with the Turners, she cooked for herself and the other performers because African Americans were not welcome in many restaurants. 'Everything was segregated back then, so there weren't many places for Black people to eat, so we had electric skillets and we'd get in our hotel rooms and cook,' she explained. Miss Robbie also sang background vocals for other artists such as Stevie Wonder and Barbra Streisand. She is now in her seventies and well-known for her soul food, which some claim to be the best in Missouri. I tried her collard greens (the best vegetables I've ever eaten) and her mac and cheese - authentic Mississippi cooking - and boasted to Miss Robbie that I make my own mac and cheese. She was extremely gracious. 'I don't want to beat you,' she explained. Simply enter me in the race!'

Australian cuisine is distinctive. In a Sydney restaurant, I tried kangaroo curry. It wasn't very good. I didn't care for the texture. Foster's lager and Vegemite, on the other hand, are food of the gods in my opinion. The 'bush tucker' or bush food, on the other hand, is a whole new level of haute cuisine. Civilisation began on a beautiful island with white sand in the far north of Australia, where you can catch and eat mud crabs, or'muddies,' according to the dreamtime culture of First Nation Tiwi people. Eleanor, a fabulous Rambling Woman, taught me how to catch muddies. You hook the crab with a stick with a barb on one end and pull it out by its shell. Eleanor also caught a dozen more mud crabs and a large blue swimmer. 'That's your lunch,' she said, and that's when I proposed to her. 'I need to marry a woman who can catch muddies in the morning,' I said. She demonstrated how to prevent the crab from nipping you with its claws by snapping two of its back legs and jamming one in each claw to prevent it from closing them. I felt sorry for them, but they were delicious little buggers. Have you ever eaten the other kind of crab? I've had boiling piss and the entire shooting match. Fucking Agghhh!!! Nothing, however, compares to crabs. When your pubic hair has turned into an adventure playground... fuuuuuck!

Eleanor's abilities were limitless. She cracked open a tree to find a worm known as a witchetty grub, which is considered a delicacy in the area. It's actually a large, white moth larva. She immediately took a couple out. They were quite long and wriggled all over the place. I ate them both alive because I'm the kind of daring savage who eats anything. A witchetty grub tastes like an oyster; it's slimy and revolting. However, when Eleanor handed me another, I ate it. Worse things have happened in my mouth. Bush tucker is very popular. It's not just the poor wretches stuck on a jungle TV show who want to try it. But I'm not sure why it's called 'bush'. Isn't it supposed to be 'The bushes?' For the love of God. It's like referring to the Sahara as "one fucking grain of sand." But what about 'the bush'? 'Oh, this must be the bush they're referring to. 'There are four million kangaroos hiding behind it.' Let's shake the bush and see what happens... They all come out boing boing...

According to Freud, whenever living creatures meet, they immediately ask, "Can I eat it?" Is it okay if I shag it? All in the blink of an eye. Alternatively, can I shag it while eating it? So, I cooked a BBQ in the woods, but it wasn't your typical backyard fare. It was a frill-necked lizard and a magpie goose leg. How fresh do you want your goose? This morning, that thing was flying. Call me old-fashioned, but if I met those animals in the bush, I'm not going to think either 'eat' or 'shag'. Eleanor possessed a wealth of knowledge. She showed me a kurrajong, which is a giant seed pod. It tastes like popcorn after being roasted in the ground. She also knew how to make baskets out of large leaves, how to wash with a soap plant, and how to grow a green plum that tastes like ginger beer. The bush is a free supermarket for First Nations people. There are shops everywhere, but everything is free and open 24 hours a day. Some of the film crew jumped in the water to swim as we walked along the beach to catch the boat back to the mainland, but they quickly came running out because one of them saw a shark. 'Shark! 'Shaaarkk!' he yelled, flailing about in the waves and teetering on the soft sand as he attempted to reach the beach. Eleanor and the other local women, on the other hand, had a completely different outlook. When they heard him yell 'Shark!' They grabbed an axe and dashed into the water. 'Shark? Where? DINNER!!!'

Eleanor's foraging abilities were not the only thing that impressed me. She had a big impact on me because she was probably the nicest person I'd ever met. Eleanor freaked out when I pointed out my daughter Cara, who was standing with the film crew at the time. She immediately ran up to her, hugged her tightly, and lavished her with affection. Later, as we were sailing back to the dock, Eleanor pointed out her son, who was waiting for her on shore. 'Look!' She was frantically informing everyone. 'Did you see him? That's my kid! My boy!' She was overjoyed for him. That type of love, demonstrative motherly love, is completely foreign to me. It makes me feel slightly uneasy... but it also has a profound effect on me. Eleanor left an indelible impression on me, and she taught me a lot.

The town of Alice Springs is in the very centre of Australia, and there's nothing else for many, many miles around it, so you have to fend for yourself without a microwave. That's where I learned how to make a damper, a swagman's traditional bread made with flour, butter, salt, and water. I'd have been fine if I'd known about the damper when I was camping in Scotland. It's a simple, delicious meal with few ingredients. Rambling Man is the traditional Australian swagger. Is this correct? He's carrying his swag, which is a rolled-up sleeping blanket. Australians used to make a lovely sleeping bag with oilskin on the outside. It has a hood that pulls up and away from your face; I've always wanted one of those. Australians do the rufty-tufty thing exceptionally well. The damper turned out great, and the entire process was thrilling. I thought I'd burned it to a crisp because the outside was all black, but when I opened the charred bit, it was delicious. I have a cookbook with a recipe for damper at home. It also includes instructions for making a purse out of a red kangaroo scrotum. Yum.

I also made Billy Tea, a traditional tea in a can, at my bush campfire. I gathered wood and started the fire - I was a Boy Scout, so I knew how to do it all from my camping days. I brewed the tea in the same can that we used in the shipyards - the one that powdered baby milk comes in. Your tea didn't taste great until the can was black. Tea from a can is fantastic tea. Simply drink it black with sugar. After that, drinking tea from a cup was always a lost cause. With my bush tea and all, the entire meal turned out to be fantastic. Then, in true Rambling Man style, I sat beneath a tree and played my autoharp. It makes a lovely sound outside.

Food can reveal a lot about a country. The pie floater is a popular delicacy in Australia. It's proper grub. None of your continental nonsense. It's essentially a meat pie with pea soup on top. You top it with brown sauce and vinegar. Someone in Australia holds the record for eating the most pie floats in three and a half hours - nine. I believe I am capable of doing so. Joe Cocker was said to always have shepherd's pie in his dressing room, except in Adelaide, where he had a pie floater.

Australian sweets are my favourite. Minties are my favourite, but they eat your fillings. Violet Crumble bars (which I call 'Violent Crumbles') and Cherry Ripes are also favourites of mine. Lamingtons are one of my favourite types of cakes. The lamington holds a special place in my heart. It's a slice of New York pizza. I'm not in New York until I've had a pizza and a Coke, and I'm not in Australia until I've had a lamington and a cup of tea. But pies are unbeatable, and I will always say 'Aye' to a pie.

Barry Humphries wrote a poem that went as follows:

I think that I could never spy,
A poem as lovely as a pie,
A banquet in a single course
Blushing with rich tomato sauce.

That's Barry. I miss him.

That was something I made up about ten years ago when I was scared on a plane and needed to distract myself.

When I've travelled, I've rarely been disappointed by the local cuisine. I travelled to Oslo to attend the Nobel Prize ceremony. That year, Nelson Mandela and F. W. de Klerk shared the Nobel Peace Prize, so I was honoured to be invited. My wife was eager to meet Mandela, so she accompanied me. We were eating reindeer for dinner at the event. 'Oh, please give us some of that!' Here's the old Rudolph and chips. So I'm eating my reindeer and wishing I had a glacé cherry to say, 'I've got the nose!' 'I have the nose!' Really screw everyone up. The room was half ANC, and most mornings in Soweto, there aren't many reindeer running around. So one half of the room was describing reindeer to the other, and they were all making antler shapes with their fingers on top of their heads... I burst out laughing. You know how your legs move? I snorted with laughter, and reindeer came down my nose. As previously stated, I dislike eating outside. There are always little annoying things buzzing around, trying to nibble on me or my food. But I make an exception for two special beach restaurants: Doyles in Watsons Bay, Sydney, and Mgarr ix-Xini in Gozo, Malta, where my friends Noel and Sandra serve the freshest, best-cooked fish I've found anywhere. Mgarr ix-Xini is a fantastic place to sit on your arse under a shady tree and pass the time while your wife goes diving, swimming around to the next bay, or climbing a sheer cliff and jumping off. Not to be outdone, I get my own workout by standing up and ordering another Cornetto. Pamela is half a woman and half a fish. There are Irish legends about silkies, which are seals who can shed their skin and transform into human women at will, and I believe she is one of them. She was born in New Zealand but is Australian. When I first moved to New Zealand, it was difficult to find food after a show. That tainted my impression of the place. I know it's not the most appropriate way to think about a country, but when you're on tour, you need basic comforts above all. During the day, if me and the crew saw a restaurant we liked, we'd go in and inquire about an evening meal. 'We finish at eight o'clock,' they'd say. 'But we start at eight!' we'd say. I didn't leave the stage until at least half past ten o'clock. They would simply shrug their shoulders. 'Good luck.' That was the case for my first few tours there. If we were lucky, the hotel restaurant would leave us a salad, but after three hours onstage, it was the last thing you wanted. And it tasted exactly like your grandmother's salad: two lettuce leaves, two slices of tomato, a boiled egg, and a smidgeon of ham. But that has all changed dramatically in the years I've been visiting New Zealand, because enterprising people have taken over the operation. A new generation has risen to power. We were eventually able to go for my favourite Indian food after the show. I recall one woman in charge of an Indian restaurant in Auckland. She served everyone and cleaned up afterwards. She was not only the cook and waiter, but she also did everything. It was so good that you wanted to give her a standing ovation after you finished your meal.

Mori people eat eel traditionally, but I've never tried it the way they do. I've never liked eel; I tried it once in London and was horrified. I despise wobbly food. I once went to a beach near the Tasman Sea to dig for TuaTuas, a type of clam, to make soup and fritters. You perform the Twist in the sand, and your bare feet will feel one of the shellfish, allowing you to pick it up and place it in your bag. New Zealand has some of the best shellfish in the world. Ian McGann, my promoter, had an aunt in Invercargill who sent us a Maxwell House jar full of oysters and green-lip mussels. Hurrah! I also enjoy the large clabby doo mussels found on Ireland's west coast. Fabulous. The best oysters I've ever had were on New Zealand's Stewart Island. When I visited Edinburgh's Mary King's Close underground street, I discovered that it was the poor who drank claret and ate oysters in the seventeenth century. It is directly beneath the City Chambers and has a terrible history; it was sealed off due to the plague and people were simply left to die there. Awful.

Some Scottish dishes are extremely addictive. I'll travel great distances for a good cullen skink, a soup made of smoked fish and potatoes. And I'm a big fan of the Arbroath smokie. It's smoked haddock, and it's fantastic. But I'm a simple man with simple tastes. I enjoy a small fairy cake and a cup of tea in the afternoon. I do, however, enjoy a small cappuccino. But I have to think 'Al Pacino' because I keep forgetting what the fucking thing's name is. I once requested a Robert De Niro. The waitress was completely perplexed.

I always asked my promoters to put nothing but a cup of tea in my dressing room, but they frequently forgot. I'd get a lot of sweets and a lot of booze. However, I enjoyed the sweets. In fact, I endorse the Mars Bar diet. If done correctly, it truly works. Some people make the mistake of eating the Mars Bar, which is incorrect. You do not consume it. You shove it up your sleeve and let a Rottweiler chase you home. On a consistent basis.

During my concerts, my audience frequently snacked on sweets. When it got too annoying, I'd single someone out and say: 'Did I hear sweeties being opened? Everything that happens in this room is MINE. That's what happens when you laugh while holding a sweetie in your mouth. And it went straight up your nose. Oh, and Coke!' 'You're going to be a big fat person.' Then someone would give me candy. 'I'm craving a chocolate eclair!' 'My personal favourite!'

I adore blueberry muffins. Definitely not bran - that's for people who are trying to starve themselves. According to my doctor, eating grapefruit burns more calories than the grapefruit itself. I recall my response clearly: 'So fucking what?' Brown bread, on the other hand, is an abomination. Brown bread is a fucking frisbee in my opinion. 'You'll live longer,' they'll say, and you will. You'll be alive for another two weeks. But it won't be the next fortnight when you're 35 and shagging like a stag. That fortnight when you're pissing your pants and being fed out of a blender and wishing you were fucking dead - that's the fortnight. You smell like piss, but you still have two weeks. 'Oh, for fuck's sake, have mercy... hit me with something,' I said. 'Throw me off the damned building!' 'No! I'll make you some brown bread!' 'Lord, have mercy! I'm fucking 97 years old!'

I'm not picky, but here are a few things that irritate me: I can't get past the stench of tripe. On my way to school, there used to be a barrow. A woman with a wheelbarrow who used to sell tripe to residents of the tenements. I despised the odour. And if someone put Brussels sprouts on my plate, I'd puke. I have a hard time eating any kind of vegetable, though I can tolerate most of them raw. I also despise rotating restaurants. They're for people who enjoy spitting after eating.

But I adore Indian cuisine. We used to have lunch in a deserted house with no roof when I was filming in India. The actors and production team ate on the first floor, which had a wide variety of food, while the crew ate on the ground floor, which only had dal and chapatis. I was heading in for lunch one day and thought to myself, 'Dal and chapatis? - 'Don't say anything else.' I went in and sat with the crew, laughing and eating my dhal. When we were about to leave, the film's manager asked, 'Have you ever been here before?' He was astounded by how easily I ate with the crew while sitting cross-legged on the floor. 'No,' I said. 'This is my first time here.' 'I think you've been here before,' he said. It gave me a chill. However, I recently discovered that my great-great-great-grandmother Matilda was Indian. Maybe that's why I react so positively to all the colours and smells of all the spices that are constantly wafting around. And then there are the intriguing Indian perfumes, which are quite different from what Europeans wear.

Madhur Jaffrey has inspired me to cook Indian food. Madhur Jaffrey is my absolute favourite. I'd like to marry her as well. I wonder if Eleanor would be interested in a little ménage à trois? My children now eat Indian food because they are adults, but they did not previously. Nothing beats a child's rejection of your food. Adults will say, 'You know, I haven't felt well all day. I'm going to go outside and get a glass of water. Do you have any paracetamol or something?' However, a child will exclaim, "Blahhhh!! No!! Dodo!!!' When my middle daughter Amy did this to me, I asked her older sister Daisy, 'What's she saying?' Daisy responded, 'She wants McDonalds.'

If I were sentenced to death, my last meal would be fish and chips. Excellent cuisine. It's a lot of fun. Haddock in the Glasgow style. Food fit for a king. Yeah, and I'd wash it down with a pint of strong. Eleanor is in charge of serving.

CHAPTER 7
PLAYING ELEPHANT POLO IN NEPAL

ONE THING AN ACTIVELY TRAVELLING RAMBLING MAN CANNOT DO EASILY IS KEEP A PET, THOUGH DOGS CAN BE ARRANGED AT TIMES. You don't find them; the dog does. Follows you around for a while before disappearing. I can't imagine attempting to board a train with one of my lazy little dogs at home. They'd sit down in protest at the crucial moment, just like they do when I walk them. 'I'm not taking it any further, Billy. You're going to have to carry me home.' If I was mugged, I'm sure they'd just roll on their backs and hope for a tummy rub. Yeah, unless you have a caravan, you can't really travel with a dog without running into courting issues. But I knew some guys who had rats. They kept them up their sleeve, with only the tail showing. They adored those rats, and they were stunning. As neat as a pin. Even though they don't usually travel with them, Rambling Men come into contact with animals on a daily basis, whether by picking up work on a farm, passing by stables, or travelling through areas teeming with all manner of creatures. Wildlife interests Rambling Men because it speaks to their inquisitive nature. One of the best towns I've ever visited was Rayne, Louisiana, which was overrun with enormous frogs. I'd never seen frogs that big before. Instead of simply trying to kill or eat them, the people of the area held a variety of events in honour of it being the frog capital of the United States. Every year, they crowned a Frog King and Queen. People really liked the frogs, with little girls dressing them up for competitions. And it was great to capture that on film and show people that hidden corner of America - the America where people don't shoot people or join the Ku Klux Klan, but instead get their frog ready for the morning. Delightful. Cows outnumber people in Texas two to one. When I was filming there, I went on a cattle drive with real modern cowboys. Baseball caps and denim. Stan, the proprietor, wore a ten-gallon hat. It's no surprise that cowboys wore bandanas when they were stuck among all those farting cows. Cows, I've heard, pollute the environment more than cars. Despite the foul odour, I felt like John Wayne riding my horse and herding the stray dogs. I imagined doing that a million times as a kid, smacking my own backside as I galloped down Hyndland Road. Cowboy movies fueled my childhood fantasies of escaping my life in Scotland to roam the prairies on a trusty steed and camp in the canyons with my posse of fellow outlaws. When I met real cowboys, they were nothing like my boyhood fantasy. In Texas, I found them to be angry and politically active people. They didn't like the fact that oil wells were being dug on their land, and they didn't like the people who protested the oil. They were on the side of no one. They didn't like lefties telling them what to do in the countryside, and they didn't like big businesses drilling holes without their permission. They used to be a stable, pleasant crowd in my memory, but if they've changed, it's understandable given how they've been messed around for years. They'd make fun of me for playing my banjo or guitar. 'Are you a cowboy, then?' 'No, I just like the music,' she says. 'Yeah. You guys are all the same...' There's a cliff. We were outsiders playing music in their town hall - music that was part of their culture, not ours. We sang about their way of life, but we weren't a part of it, and we weren't one of them. They have every right to feel that way. It didn't seem to matter that we were there because we loved the music and admired them; we were just fashionistas, glitzy, showbiz rhinestone cowboys to them. I once wrote my own comedy version of 'Rhinestone Cowboy,' which went something like this:

I'm a half-stoned cowboy,
Who fell off on his arse in the middle of the rodeo,
Just a half-stoned cowboy,
Buying beer and whiskey for people I don't even know,
And I wonder where my money goes.
I was having a drink alone,
When someone called me to the phone,
He was making a joke about trouble that was coming my way,
It was my wife saying what's your game,
You know you ought to be bloody ashamed the way you carry on,
You got a load of children starving,
And a jungle that once was a garden,
And you're off like a shot every night as far as I can see.
(Everybody! . . .) Like a half-stoned cowboy . . .

Perhaps the cowboys I met had done their homework. Perhaps they were wary of me because I had previously made jokes about them. Onstage, I used to make a train whistle sound and say, "That's a lonely whistle." Cowboys like them when they're guarding the steers at night on the prairie. Singing songs in the midst of a raging Apache. Eating beans and farting everywhere. A lonely whistle in the distance reminds them of their true love who is far away. They shed a silent tear before crawling into bed and interfering with themselves. Cowboys have very short vision.'

The first time I rode a horse for real was for a TV show in which celebrities were taught to do things they had never done before. I learned to ride a horse while one of the guys learned to hang glide. I visited some opulent stables in Kingston-upon-Thames. The horse stood on my foot the first day. I'll never forget how painful it was. I had no idea how close or far you could get to a horse. She was a lovely horse, a magnificent gold-coloured mare, but I believe she could spot a rookie. She bit me once. I was standing outside her door, which was one of those half-doors. And she leaned over and, for no apparent reason, bit my shoulder. 'Get out of it!' I said sternly, and she never came near me again in a malicious manner. I sat on the horse for the first time inside the riding school, while my trainer led us in a circle. I eventually progressed to riding around the park and across the pond. The water reached her knees. Then we did some jumping. That was difficult because I couldn't keep my bum under control. When you're jumping and flying, you should stick your bum out backwards. It was awkward at first, but I eventually got the hang of it. One day, I slapped the horse's neck. "We don't slap horses' necks here," said the trainer. Cowboys do that in cowboy movies. You are welcome to pat her.' What I remember most is walking through the woods and seeing squirrels on trees just staring at you - they didn't run away because you were a horse, not a guy. It was fantastic. When I learned to trot and canter through the park, I was deemed ready for filming, so a crew arrived to film me riding through the New Forest National Park near Southampton. It's a training facility for wild forest ponies. Some become working ponies, while others simply roam the forest eating grass and fucking around. It's nothing like the Kingston stables. Agisters are the people who look after them. I was standing there talking to my horse one day when she bit me. The second horse, the second nip. 'Don't let her do that!' said one of the agisters as she punched the horse in the face. 'Oh, this isn't Kingston,' I thought. The horse exclaimed, 'Oh fuck.' I took the lesson very seriously. 'Get on.' said the agister. I got on the horse. 'What have you done?' he asked. 'I've trotted and cantered and jumped a little,' I explained. 'Not a lot.' 'Come on, we'll see,' he said. And he slapped his horse on the neck, and we shot up a hill together. It was thrilling. Through the trees and up to the top of the hill. Swishhhh! and he hit it again. That's when my horse turned into a cylinder. My legs were crossed beneath her. I had the sensation that I was on a wild rocket ship. We rode along to where the other horses began to appear, and by the time we got close to the park's end, there were about forty horses everywhere. They began running alongside us, yelling, 'Ayeeeghhh! Ayeee Ghh!' Neighbours yelling and making a commotion. Now I was living my rambling cowboy fantasy. We were moving like a freight train. Then we descended a hill, and as we gained speed, I noticed a branch about the height of the horse approaching us. They had warned me about it at the riding school, so I just laid back on the horse's back and went under the branch, and the people from Kingston exclaimed, 'Woohoo!!' I felt like a ruffian stuntman. The next time I rode a horse was for the film The Last Samurai, starring Tom Cruise. Sergeant Zebulon Gant, an Irish American Civil War veteran, was the character I played. 'Can you ride a horse?' they asked. I replied, 'Yes.' They asked, 'Can you do military stuff?' and I said, 'Yes,' despite the fact that I had no idea what they were talking about. It was simple. All I had to do was keep my horse walking in the same direction as the other guys. That was something the horses enjoyed doing. We had to keep them calm and prevent them from panicking as we rode alongside a burning building. I had to ride down the hill with several of the men to the 'headquarters' while holding fire weapons. 'Stand your ground!' I had to yell during the battle scenes. 'Return fire!' the men yelled as samurai attacked them through the trees. That was frightening. My horse, fortunately, liked me. We shot everything in New Zealand, and I got to go fishing in the middle of it all. Yippee! What was the sweetest thing I did in New Zealand? I let out a small kiwi into the wild. It dashed into a safe haven where none of its predators could find it. Delightful. That's me, Kiwi Whisperer. It was a delight to watch it scoot away. I've had amazing encounters with all kinds of animals, including koalas, wombats, and penguins. I'm the comedy equivalent of Joy Adamson. I was walking down a cobblestone street in Malta when I heard a fast clippity clop behind me. A quick clippity clop. When I turned around, there was a man working out his racehorse by holding the reins out the back of a moving station wagon. I was laughing so hard that I peed myself. That was the first time I'd seen anything like it. They practise controlling their speed - twenty miles per hour, twenty-five miles per hour, whatever - as they drive down long straight roads. He was offended because I was laughing. 'You fucking Scottish jerk!'

As I was reminded at the Payson Rodeo in Texas, animal control is frequently a lost cause. It was terrifying. The first person I spoke with was a seasoned rodeo rider. 'I used to work as a bull rider,' he explained. 'However, three broken necks later...' He told me that bulls are extremely intelligent animals. 'They learn your moves the first time you ride them, and they're way ahead of you after that. Know all of your gimmicks. 'It's like climbing into a ring with Muhammad Ali,' says the man who weighs 17 hundred pounds. It's a difficult life. Rodeo riders must travel hundreds of miles and then pay to compete. And they don't get paid if they don't win. I met a lady who claimed to be the 'Rodeo Queen' and World Champion Barrel Racer. That made no sense to me. She explained that the competing riders raced their horses around three barrels arranged in a triangle formation in the arena. They were incredibly skilled at it. They say you have to 'ride it like you stole it!' I went like the clappers. The rodeo performances included people of all ages. I witnessed a five-year-old performing crazy rodeo moves on a hyperactive sheep, only to be thrown off. Brutal. In 1968, a ten-year-old named 'Annie the Okie' won a barrel racing competition but died before receiving the gold buckle. She was killed in a highway traffic accident between Little Rock, Arkansas and Waco, Texas on her way to a rodeo event. When you try out new skills while filming TV shows, you can really get exposed. I tried archery in preparation for going hunting but only managed to hit a plastic moose in the arse. My hunting guides, twin sisters Sherry and Caroline, arrived at 5 a.m. the next day to take me turkey hunting. I'd never hunted wild turkey before, but I was dressed to kill in my full-body camouflage. When we arrived at the hide, I embarrassed myself yet again by laughing when one of the twins made a very realistic turkey call to attract their prey. They collaborated: Sherry used a call to entice them, and Caroline used her bow to shoot them. At least, that was the theory. It was a little suffocating in the hide. My bed had been extremely warm. Dawn broke... and there was still nothing. Turkey sandwiches were no longer available. To be honest, I was relieved they got away.

During my train tour, I saw American buffalo. I adore them. They have enormous heads. When you approach them, they're covered in flies. You wave your arms and they fly away, thinking you're doing the buffalo a favour, but it actually enjoys having the flies around. They're covered in small birds that eat their parasites when you see them in Africa. Buffalo are beautiful animals, but they can be arrogant. They get nosy when you're fishing and come along to check you out. They have been known to turn people on their heads. The buffalo came down while I was fishing with my son Jamie in Yellowstone National Park. 'Watch them, they're a little... territorial,' people warned us. Beautiful-looking creatures. I wish I had gone on safari when I travelled in Africa because I would have seen more wildlife. Quite the contrary. The only animals I saw the first time I was in Biafra for work - I was a welder at the time - were men who'd been on a dry oil rig all week, at a bar on a Friday night. I include myself in this. The other times I was in Africa, I was there to film for Comic Relief, and there were far more important things to focus on than going on a safari. I got the idea to talk about wildebeest and lions in my concerts after watching wildlife documentaries on television. They were fantastic. My hero is Sir David Attenborough. I appeared on Parkinson's show a couple of times. He once came on the show, sat down to talk about a new bird show he'd done, and turned to me and asked, 'Do you know about Penduline tits?' I gave him a sidelong glance and asked, 'Are you offering me something here?' He burst out laughing. Another time, he told a story about going to the bathroom in a foreign country and finding a rat between his legs. 'I hate it when that happens,' I said, and he just lost it. I was singing a song after the show, and we danced up the stairs together. What a life he's led!

I did meet some African wild dogs at a wolf sanctuary in Missouri, where I fed them pigs' ears and a rat. They saved the rat's tail for last because it's apparently the best part. Those dogs are incredible creatures. They share their food, and when they go hunting in a pack, they leave a babysitter to look after their young. They regurgitate to feed not only their babies but also the babysitter when they return.

The sanctuary existed because wolves were almost extinct in the area at the time. The keepers were careful not to pet, talk to, or play with the wolves because they were committed to keeping them wild and fearful of humans for their own protection. I went into the wolves' enclosure and assisted in feeding them a deer. One of the wolves had unusual table manners. He peed on the food first, which could have been his way of defrosting it. Many African animals end up in private hands in the United States; in fact, I was told there was a $50 billion-dollar illegal industry involving at least 15,000 big cats. I believe Americans only discovered this after the television series Tiger King became popular. I once encountered a rescued baby tiger. Anthony was his name, and he was fed from a bottle. Illegally kept animals include monkeys, llamas, lions, and tigers, all of which are dangerous pets. I heard about a monkey that bit the owner's girlfriend's ear off. I'm perfectly content with my three adorable puppies. Some wild animals seek out humans simply because they can. Manatees are frequently seen in the shallow seas and canals where I live in the Florida Keys. They bask and play, eat seagrass, and drink freshwater run-off. They are fantastic. They're incredibly friendly, despite the fact that you're not supposed to interact with them. They occasionally pass by my dock with babies and look at me as if to say, 'Meet my new wean!' And in affluent areas of America with heated pools, hot tubs, and jacuzzis, people are constantly posting stories and videos of bears climbing into and relaxing in the warm water, particularly in the Great Smoky Mountains. A bear was spotted in a hot tub by a man in Altadena, California. It started out just relaxing, but then it started messing around with his chlorinator and tossing the thermometer around. Then it galloped over to a half-finished margarita on a garden table, knocked it over, and drank it down. When I visit the Florida Keys, I see a lot of unusual animals that most Glaswegians never see in person. Iguanas irritate many Floridians because they spit all over your yard, eat your flowers, and can be dangerous to pets. I, on the other hand, adore them. They have stunning colouring, particularly the large, bright-orange males. When tropical storms or hurricanes knock down trees, they become disoriented. Alpha iguanas live on the highest branches in their society, but when they are broken off, their world is turned upside down. You can see them wandering around aimlessly after a big storm, having lost their status as top-branch dwellers. The Florida Keys are teeming with chickens. Because they are a protected species, you may not catch or eat them. The roosters are especially stunning, with iridescent feathers that catch the light. People are constantly forced to stop their vehicles for chicken families. Why do chickens in the Florida Keys cross the road? To irritate motorists. In south Florida, you'll see road signs with pictures of crocodiles or alligators. You are not given any additional information. But it would be interesting to know if those reptiles like to take a stroll around there, or if they're looking for lost motorists. I understand that entering an animal's habitat invites trouble, but many animals appear to believe that they can enter ours without incident. During Comic Relief filming, I was in an AIDS ward in Mozambique, Africa. I went back to see how a guy we had filmed a few days earlier was doing. A goat came in and pissed against his bedside table while I was talking to him, then walked out. In addition, I saw a giraffe at Nairobi International Airport. The park is situated near the airport. 'Look,' I said to the taxi driver. 'It's a giraffe!!' He just said 'Yeah?' as if I'd pointed out a pigeon. Pigs were never my favourite animals. They strike me as quite vicious. I was bitten by a pig once while trying to be nice to it... despite being in its pen. But I've grown very fond of some animals. At home, I adore my small dogs. I also liked Ralph McTell's parrot. Albert was the best talking parrot I'd ever seen. 'Good morning, Bill!' If you shook your keys, he'd ask, 'Is that you away, then?' 'What do you have to do to get a drink around here?' he'd ask if the atmosphere was quiet. When Albert began coughing, Ralph became extremely concerned. Ralph took him to the vet because he made a deathly rattle. The vet examined Albert and said, 'I hate to tell you, Ralph, but that's YOUR cough!' He's copying you. Your parrot is perfectly healthy, but you'll have to deal with your own cough...'

Australian animals terrify me to death. They have a greater variety of creepy-crawlies than anywhere else on the planet. I've had a few spider bites. I had a sore on the inside of my leg and had no idea what caused it. It turned out that some vicious little bastard had sunk its fangs into my leg without my knowledge. It needed to be drained and looked after. Perth, Western Australia, was the location. Pamela came in and threw a Mintie at me while the doctor was giving it to me. She probably thought she was cheering me up, but I was in excruciating pain. She claimed it was the local spider bite treatment. She grew up with deadly spiders in her backyard, so it felt like removing a splinter. My arachnophobia is frequently underestimated by those around me, but not by my Australian promoter, Kevin. When I got out of the car to go to a gig, there was a spider on my shoulder. Kevin grabbed it in a flash. I didn't see it or I'd have passed out. Another time, I was climbing down the exterior stairs of a house in Pearl Beach, running my hand down the bannister, when the wee bastard bit me from beneath. He viciously attacked me. I was convinced that I was going to die. Aussies live in a paradise, but they have a lot of horrible creepy-crawlies. They're all over. Any country with a poisonous spider lurking in the restroom waiting for you to sit is a dangerous place. Being bitten on the scrotum isn't my idea of a good time. Alternatively, anywhere in the genolica area. 'Doctor, you're never going to believe this...' I also saw an Australian woman on a nature show. She had funnel web spiders as pets. They are the spider world's Glaswegian tough men. Aggressive and dangerous. She seemed to enjoy this spider. 'He's nice,' she said. Fuck. Consider him standing on his hind legs and saying, 'C'mere!' Imagine his fangs sinking into one of your testicles as you sleep. But my favourite Australian animals are the kangaroos and koalas. They're gorgeous, and they apparently taste good. The koala, not so much. While driving to Iron Knob, I saw kangaroos in the outback. We were driving along when kangaroos began to hop alongside us. Why? I'm not sure. It was similar to dolphins tailing your boat or wild horses tailing our car in Montana. Perhaps the kangaroos thought we'd feed them, like the monkeys at Windsor Safari Park who used to climb on your car and rip off your windscreen wipers. Anyway, whatever they desired, I thought it was incredible to witness. I had never seen a live kangaroo before. The wombat is my favourite animal on the planet. I first saw a wombat on a television show. He was a hairy-nosed wombat, and I thought that was the most beautiful name I'd ever heard for a creature. Later, I met some people in Australia who said they had a pet wombat who was a real annoyance. He dug huge holes in the garden, which enraged them because he never returned through the same hole - he always dug a new one. Their backyard was a maze of underground passageways. But the creature's oddity piqued my interest. Wombats, like kangaroos, have a small pocket, but the opening is near their legs, so it doesn't fill up with dirt when they dig. My first encounter with a live wombat was in a television studio with his zookeeper, and I was allowed to pet him. He was the size of a large mouse. I'd never seen one in the wild, but I had a stuffed wombat named Wally that I loved. I saw a few in the zoo, and I really wanted to get close to one called 'Digger,' but they said he was a vicious bugger. Another smaller guy was dubbed 'Not So' because he lacked the hair that the others possessed. Really? They must have stayed up all night coming up with these names.

I like platypus because they have features that shouldn't be together. This appears to be a design flaw. A creature that lays eggs, fights with its claws, and carries poison on its back? However, I've never seen one in the wild. Nowadays, I enjoy drawing strange creatures, possibly inspired by the platypus. I created the Gozunder Fish, which has a unicorn horn and a platypus tail-shaped leg, and I drew 'Run to the Fly,' another odd fish with two legs. My parents used to call me "Up a gum tree." I had no idea what it meant, but I could tell it wasn't good. I now think it's fantastic. I'd like to be up there with the koalas, stoned and shagging all hours of the day and night. Koalas are the animal hippies. Rottnest Island is an island near Perth that I visited. I flew with a film crew there. It was a bumpy flight, and I got sick all over my jacket and the microphone on the way. The consummate professional, as always. On Rottnest Island, you can see these little creatures known as quokkas. When some Dutch explorers saw them in the eighteenth century, they thought they were rats, but they were actually small marsupials. Tourists try to take selfies with them because the structure of their faces makes them appear to be smiling. They are very friendly and unafraid of humans, so getting a quokka selfie isn't too difficult - though they can bite. Unfortunately, they are sometimes fed chips, which are extremely unhealthy for them. Fraser Island is another Australian island that I visited. They have Australia's purest breed of dingoes. They were visible at Eastern Beach, where all of the roads are made of sand. I sat under a tree, watching the sunset and playing my banjo, surrounded by dingoes. Heaven. Being a Rambling Man on the road can be hell on occasion.

Animals have no concept of the month. March flies irritated me once while I was filming outside in Australia. Nightmare. They were diving bombing me and biting the s*** out of me. 'It's not March, it's fucking November!' I wanted to scream at one of them. They should do a calendar airdrop. Several flying objects landed on my tits while I was filming. When I was doing a TV presentation in Cardiff Bay, the birds were squawking so loudly that we had to come to a halt. To keep the birds from spitting on the statues, they were all wired up. To be honest, I believe it is a bird's duty to spit on people and monuments. During one of my American tours, I took a riverboat down the Mississippi, and I'm glad I did. The river was lovely. Huge. I sailed on the delta first, then deviated to a wonderful bayou - a tributary teeming with jumping fish... and snappy monsters. I'm starting to like crocodiles. There are a few near my home in the Florida Keys. Chris, a friend of mine, is an expert at catching and relocating them. They're shy creatures, unlike the ferocious salties you get in Australia who will chase you down the street the moment they see you. People in the Keys, on the other hand, don't like it when docile crocodiles come into their yards and eat their pets, or when they make a home in storm drains and refuse to leave. Some even lie across the airport tarmac, preventing planes from taking off, which is bad for tourism. Then Chris appears, lures them with a tasty dead thing, captures them, humanely ties them up, and loads them into his truck. He brings them home and plays loud heavy metal music to them all night to remind them not to approach humans, then drives them up to the Everglades or somewhere far away to release them into their new home. Excellent strategy. Northern Australians attract large reptiles by dangling pig heads and eye fillets from a pole. This was on the banks of the Adelaide River on the outskirts of Kakadu National Park. A large crocodile approached. His name was Nick. He was particularly fond of his eye fillet. People drew him closer to the bank, and I tried out the pole. He came half-way out of the water to grab it. Jaws open extremely wide. He's been around for two hundred million years. You get pretty good at what you do in 200 million years - and you'd be good at anything in another 200 million years. In 200 million years, I'm sure I'll be able to play the banjo properly. They installed a swimming pool off the beach in Cairns, Australia's north-east coast, that was designed to float in the sea. It was thought to be the only way to swim in the sea without being eaten by a saltwater crocodile. They launched it with great fanfare... but the next morning's local newspaper featured a picture of a crocodile climbing into it. Brilliant. Of course, my Arctic Circle adversary, the polar bear, is thought to be one of the most intelligent creatures on the planet. They are incredible animals, but do they have internet access? No. So they can't be that astute. Sea creatures are intelligent creatures. The people in charge of an aquarium in Auckland told me that they'd had some crayfish in a tank across from this octopus's tank, and they were mysteriously disappearing. They tried a variety of methods to figure out what was going on and eventually discovered that this cunning octopus was sneaking out of his tank at night and the octopus was singing his way into the crayfish tank and eating them. The next day, he appeared very content. An octopus can apparently fit through a hole the size of a twenty-pence piece. But don't you adore them? The most amazing creatures. Three hearts are found in an octopus. You can break his heart twice and he'll still be in love with you. There are also eight tentacles. When I was a kid, I thought it was testicles. 'Those buggers must have a scrotum like a bag of potatoes,' I reasoned. They also have suckers that you can't get away from. They have the ability to drag you into a cave and shag you senseless. Man and the sea-beast are constantly at odds. For instance, the stonefish appears to be a stone, lying in the sand and saying, 'Stand on me - I'm just a wee stone.' But if you stand on this thing, they say you'll experience the most agonising pain known to man. I'll never know how they know. Perhaps they have a pain-metre. Is there a metre that goes from 'Ouch' to 'WTF'? 'Jesus Christ!' to 'Sweet Mother of Jesus' to 'Agony' to 'Worst Pain Known to Man?' 'Fuck! It's completely out of this world!'

During my first trip to New Zealand in the late 1970s, I read in the newspaper about an incident that occurred during a family cricket game by the sea. They'd made a wicket out of three large twigs in the sand. The ball fell into the water at one point, and the kids ran in after it, but then someone noticed an approaching shark. The father of one of the children dashed into the water. The waves were crashing over his head, but his arse was a blur. This man got in between the shark and his son and hit the shark across the face with a cricket bat. When I heard that, I thought to myself, 'I like it here.' It was the kind of thing I used to see in British comic books when I was a kid: crazy, heroic acts. They should make movies about him.

I'm relieved that not all sea creatures are dangerous. The Auckland Aquarium has some adorable penguins. I entered their enclosure and sat beside them; they were quite friendly. Fatboy was the name of one of them. He was in charge. What a ruckus! He sang me a song! And in Western Australia, I fulfilled a lifelong dream by swimming with wild dolphins. But I was concerned that there might be other things lurking around the dolphin. Sharks don't charge into

Woolworths and bite you on the backside when you're minding your own business, do they? Where was the person when you heard on the news, 'A shark ate a person last week'? - in the middle of the sea! You're in their territory, after all. But I got up at 7 a.m., which is the middle of the night in my opinion, and went in the sea anyway. I rented an underwater scooter and went swimming with wild dolphins. It was incredible. Beyond comprehension. My 53rd birthday had arrived. I got a cake with a picture of myself swimming with dolphins on it! I couldn't have asked for a better birthday present, because as a kid, I imagined myself as Jacques Cousteau. He was the original underwater Rambling Man to me, roaming the oceans, discovering extraordinary things and surviving solely on his wits. He invented equipment that allowed him to explore parts of the sea that no one had previously imagined - a Rambling Man giant. Unfortunately, my early attempts to follow in his footsteps as a scuba diver revealed that I was better off staying topside due to my inability to focus on important things like how much air I had left.

Australia has to be the luckiest country on the planet. When one of their prime ministers was allegedly eaten by a shark, people in the United Kingdom wondered, 'Why didn't we think of that? We had to put up with Margaret Thatcher for years - and all those sharks doing nothing...' There's a lot of advice out there for avoiding sharks. In Australia, people say, 'If a shark gets too nosy, punch it on the nose.' 'If a shark bites you, it's just mistaken identity,' he adds. It'd take one bite and then spit it out.' Screw that! My arse has vanished...

Sharks abound in Sydney Harbour. I took a ride across the harbour on 'the Bounty,' a replica sailing ship built for the Mel Gibson film. It was lovely to play my banjo on board. Pamela scolded me for mispronouncing Vaucluse, where an eccentric Irish baron named Henry Browne Hayes was brought as a convict for kidnapping a Quaker heiress. He was terrified of snakes, so he brought 300 barrels of peat from Ireland and placed it around his Vaucluse home, believing that no snake would dare to cross a piece of Irish 'Holy Land' (it was believed that St Patrick had banished snakes from Ireland). But an area of Australia devoid of snakes? Not very likely. Australian snakes can also surprise you. Bastards. Personally, I like the American rattlesnake better. It may be camouflaged, but it is the only snake in the world that will alert you to its presence. I'll give you a heads up. Sssscchhhhlackleacklackle means 'Don't make any sudden movements.' We passed Fort Denison on the Bounty, a sturdy stone island fortress built to protect the harbour. It was built incorrectly, and when it was finished, they discovered that it couldn't fire muskets or guns! I admire the human race. Such delightful stupidity! We also passed Goat Island, which was once a small penal island. Charlie Anderson, a prisoner from Glasgow, made it famous. He was making such a nuisance of himself by constantly attempting to flee that he was sentenced to two years chained to a rock. The other inmates carved him a couch on the rock, which is now known as Charlie Anderson's Couch. His chain was 26 feet long, and when people sailed by, he would yell at them. 'Fuck yourselves!' This is a man after my own heart. They were so terrified of him that they fed him with a long pole. When it comes to long poles, I have little interest in polo, but when my manager said, 'How would you like to go to Nepal and play polo on an elephant?' I jumped at the chance. 'I was about to ask you if I could do that,' I explained. I asked, 'What are you fucking talking about?' He laughed. 'It has come up,' he said. Someone has withdrawn; would you like to fill in?' 'I'd love to go to Nepal,' I said. When I arrived at the famous Tiger Tops hotel, I discovered that, despite the fact that we were supposed to be provided with polo equipment, there was none for me, and my luggage had been stolen in India, so I had nothing. Everyone else was dressed up in smart breeches and high polo boots, but I was stuck in khakis and desert boots. We went to the polo field the next day. It was in the Himalayan foothills, with breathtaking scenery all around. I remember being taken aback. 'Look at that!' I said to one of the guys who knew what he was talking about when I saw one of the mountains. It's right next to us!' 'It's a long way away,' he said. Because of its size, I assumed it was only a few steps away. The celebrity team consisted of myself, Ringo Starr and his wife Barbara Bach, Steve Strange, and Max Boyce - what a strange group of people! The other team was made up of real polo players, Nepalese guys who worked for Nepal's King Mahendra. He was the one who hosted the Cartier-sponsored game. I believe he simply enjoyed holding celebrity matches for no apparent reason. He owned the elephants. The other team, understandably, despised us because we knew nothing about polo and even less about elephants. I was instructed to mount my elephant, but no one showed me how, so I improvised. I charged at it from behind, jumped on it, and placed my feet behind its head - I knew you did that last part. But then the mahut, the guy in charge of my elephant, hit the elephant in the head with a file. 'Hey, no more,' I said. 'Don't fuck up with that!' Then one of the bosses came over and mumbled something. 'He's a townie,' he was probably saying. He knows fuck everything about it.' But I was aware that you do not hit animals in the head with files. Later, I was riding my elephant, and a guy was collecting my elephant's shit in a big sheet, and he told me, 'It's a normal job here.' 'No, it's a nail-biting cure,' I replied. They liked me and I liked them from then on. A sense of humour can always help to break the ice. In the end, we were defeated. Of course we did, because none of us knew what we were doing. Nobody really showed us anything. 'That's your pole,' they said. This is the ball. Hit the ball with the pole towards the goal. Don't be alarmed if the elephants become overly excited. They'll stand on their hind legs and make a huge racket, but you'll grow to love it. It was correct. When the elephants were running for the ball, they yelled "Bahooooooo!! Bahooooo!!" My elephant would rear up on its hind legs like the old circus elephants, but I was securely fastened to it by a rope that wrapped around my lap, under my thighs, and around its belly. I had to tell the mahut which way to go because he was in front of me, further up the elephant's neck. He was in charge of the steering. Finally, we were awarded large sums of money. I received a lovely ashtray. That was the end of it. They took us out into the jungle the day after the match, but we hadn't been there long when the guide abruptly stopped. 'I can detect the scent of a female tiger. She is close.' 'Well, why the fuck are we still here?' I asked. We made a quick retreat. Later that day, I came across a baby rhinoceros. It was breathtaking, following its mother through the elephant grass. Then we got off the elephants and were drinking tea when I noticed a rabbit. 'Oh my God, look, a rabbit!' I exclaimed. Finally, something that isn't going to eat you.' But as I approached it, it scurried away, and I exclaimed, 'Fucking hell! That's no rabbit!' Its legs were the size of my fingers. It was the largest, most terrifying spider I'd ever seen.

CHAPTER 8
PLAYING BANJO WITH THE LESBIAN MERMAIDS

In the late sixties, it was fashionable to be a certain type of Rambling Man - a hippy version. When I was still a welder, I was watching a BBC program called Tonight with Cliff Michelmore, and they had a segment about a phenomenon happening in St Ives, Cornwall. All these hairy people had moved there, living in caravans and cottages. They'd formed a community and were having a great time playing music. I was completely captivated by it, particularly by one of their leaders, Wizz Jones, a singer-songwriter with a beard and hair halfway down his back who was playing the blues exceptionally well. When I met him years later and told him he was an inspiration to me, he laughed. 'I got letters from everywhere, from people complaining that their sons were negatively influenced by me,' he said. So I wasn't the only one thinking to myself, 'How can I get to look like that and play like that?' He was an exceptional guitarist. It was inspiring to see people doing what I had hoped to do, such as Alex Campbell, Ralph McTell, and Clive Palmer of the Incredible String Band. They were busking and sometimes doing the clubs, protesting against steady jobs. They had made a firm decision to live a different lifestyle than most other people, and I admired them for it. I coveted it for myself.

Bert Jansch was another Rambling Man who I admired at the time. He wrote great songs and rose to international fame, with devoted fans all over the world. He was a friend of Ralph McTell's, and I first met him in a folk club in the 1960s. He was a loner who did not feel at ease in the company of others. Women adored him, and I did, too. He was thrown, which is the Scottish word for "gaunt." His cheekbones stood out. Thrawn is a better term. He once told me something about himself that absolutely floored me. He said he'd heard the great guitarist Davey Graham had been in North Africa - in Morocco - playing guitar and picking up on local Arabic music. Bert then decided he wanted to go to Morocco as well. He went and wore a duffle coat the entire time he was there. That was it for the story. I almost fell out of my chair. He was a Rambling Man folk singer in a duffle coat in Morocco. He was so foolish. 'I was roasting, but I didn't want to take off my duffle coat,' he said. 'It's a nice coat.' Bert and I met for the last time in Aberdeen. I saw him on the street. He was performing at a venue called the Lemon Tree when he announced, 'I just got married.' I asked, 'Are you kidding me?' He replied, 'Yeah. That's my wife. We got married on the Isle of Arran.' If you go to a folk singer-songwriter concert, you will hear at least one song about love on the road. 'I ran into her on the road.' Or 'I miss her... I was on the road.' It's a distinctive way of life.

Many of the guys I've met in bands fit the Rambling Man description. Being in a band is a Rambling Man subset - going on tour and doing something your parents knew nothing about and didn't understand. The majority of folk singers were Rambling Men. They'll sing about being able to get away from their problems by finding freedom on the road, meeting other people who share their feelings, and stopping being miserable. Many of Bob Dylan's songs are about being on the road and meeting people on the road, being disappointed in love on the road...

When your rooster crows at the crack of dawn

Look out your window, and I'll be gone.

You are the reason I am travelling.

People who are purely songwriters are not usually Rambling Men; making a living writing songs is something entirely different. We may want to write songs, but we don't necessarily want to make a living doing so. Our songs are simply precious expressions of our lives that are not intended to be commercially successful.

Rambling Men are common in rock 'n' roll. Not so much the stars; they have a job that requires them to go on tour and then return home. However, the crew frequently switches from one long tour with one band to another with a different band. They've chosen this rambling lifestyle. Some do not have homes and instead stay with friends or family when they visit their hometowns. There are some notable Rambling Men, such as Davey Johnstone, who played guitar in Elton John's band. I first met him when we were both younger. We slept on people's floors while performing in clubs with the Incredible String Band. It was beautiful. We didn't stay in one place for too long, as is typical of Rambling Man.

I knew Ralph McTell was a fellow Rambling Man the moment I met him. He sang wonderful songs about searching, longing, and discovery while playing acoustic guitar. I became his friend, which was a wonderful thing to be a friend of a genuine guy. We were on the same wavelength. Ralph wrote and sang the wonderful song 'Streets of London,' which serves as a Rambling Man anthem.

In the 1960s and 1970s, the romantic nature of the Rambling Man became part of the zeitgeist. There was a sense of longing, and sometimes, as in Tom Paxton's lyrics for 'Ramblin' Boy,' a sense of steadfast loyalty, camaraderie, and loss:

He was a man and a friend always.
He stuck with me in the bad old days,
He never cared if I had no dough,
We rambled around in the rain and snow.

Woody Guthrie was the emperor of the Rambling Men, and Tom Waits was the king. They even made it a lucrative lifestyle while presenting themselves as simple rambling folkies. We were all on the outskirts of it - I was no Woody Guthrie in my folk-singing days.

I had loved American country music since I was a child, and even though many of the really big country music stars, such as Glen Campbell, Johnny Cash, Dolly Parton, and Bobby Vee, didn't seem like Rambling Men because what we knew about their lives was fed through well-oiled career operations and all about People magazine, mansions, red carpets, and the Grand Ole Opry, I and other Rambling Men enjoyed their music because they sang about life and disappointment and joy - They did sometimes take the tragic element a little too far, which is why I've made fun of country singers a lot. I've even devised a formula for crafting a truly tragic country song. What you need are relatives, the closer the better, so get your mother in there. And God should make an appearance, as well as a disaster or two, as many as you want. Someone in it should have something terrible wrong with them, preferably a terminal disease. I wrote a country and western song that was completely inappropriate. It was, after all, sick. It was titled 'My Mother Drowned in the Grotto at Lourdes Because a Hunchback Pushed Her In'. I showed it to my publisher, who told me, "You'll never get away with that, Bill, it's a disgrace." Bill, you require medical attention. It's infuriating.' So I changed the title to 'How Can I Tell You I Love You When You're Sitting on My Face?'

When Rambling singers sang about love, they weren't talking about long-term monogamous relationships. 'We're going to the chapel to get married...' none of that. It was never about marriage - that was the end of it all. Rambling Man songs were still about love, but they were more often about fleeting, fleeting experiences. They were about freedom, longing, and meeting a variety of people along the way who you could fall in love with for a while. But not indefinitely. Along with this movement, the social landscape was changing. You could even dress like each other. I once swapped pants with a guy on an Amsterdam bridge. That's perfectly normal. See, looking good was important early on. It was critical to wear the right jeans, such as Levi's 501s. I was probably a little too fashionable for my own good; when I first wore flares, people called me Popeye. We wanderers dressed in desert boots, cowboy boots, denim and cheesecloth shirts. We wore donkey jackets, motorcycle leathers, corduroy jackets, and scarves and beads as outerwear. I used to dab sandalwood oil on myself, and I used to wear patchouli oil until I was thrown out of a Quebec pub for wearing it. 'You stink like dog piss.'

The guitar you played was also important in the 1960s and 1970s. There were fashionable and unfashionable guitars. Someone would say, 'See, so-and-so's fine, but he plays a Welsh guitar.' Snobbery. A Martin was the best guitar to own. Gerry Rafferty misplaced my guitar on the train and has yet to apologise. It was a Harmony Sovereign - a fantastic instrument. Gerry didn't have a guitar at the time... well, he did have a guitar, but it had been painted by the artist John Byrne, and Gerry didn't want to take it on the road. I lent him my guitar out of kindness, and he left it on a train. Bastard.

Ukuleles were not considered trendy. Those who possessed them were regarded as mere plinky-plonky players incapable of expressing the same high emotions as guitarists - love, regret, and longing. We thought of them as pains in the arse, just like people who played bongos. However, many people feel the same way about banjo players. Eric Idle, a friend of mine, once said, 'Banjo - the musical choice of the antisocial.' He's correct, and I knew from the start of my fascination with the banjo that it wasn't always a popular instrument, but I didn't care. I've been fascinated by the noise it makes since I was a child. I've also dabbled in the ukulele and love my autoharp, which is an easily controlled instrument that sounds lovely with the acoustic voice. Because my Parkinson's disease makes it difficult for my left hand to do what my brain tells it to do, I've started playing my harmonica more and more. It's great for playing blues, in particular. The harmonica is popular in the Rambling Man universe. It has a plaintive sound and fits easily into your pocket.

Music is important to many Rambling Men because it is an artistic form of expression that can be taken with you wherever you go. You must select your instrument carefully; there is a reason why there are no cello-playing Rambling Men. I've amassed a nice collection of instruments over the years, but it pales in comparison to a musical instrument collection I saw near Springfield, Illinois. The owner, Rob, had the most impressive, eclectic collection of musical instruments I could have imagined, including the world's largest collection of lap steels. He owned just under 2,000 electric guitars and also collected zithers and ukuleles. All of this was displayed on the walls of the man's massive, secret space. He wasn't a dealer or anything; it was simply his personal collection. He never made a sale. He told me he also collects oddities like tweed suitcases and medicine bottles. He describes himself as an obsessive-compulsive, manic-depressive collector. I appreciate the fact that he and his collection exist in the world.

My fascination with folk-style musical instruments dates back to my childhood and my heritage. I have Irish ancestry. My Connolly ancestors are from the west coast of Ireland, while my MacLeans ancestors are from the west coast of Scotland. I get a tingling sensation whenever I visit these coastal areas of Ireland and Scotland. It feels like home to me. Our culture is inextricably linked to music. There are many gatherings of people in Ireland who just get together privately, or in pubs or halls, to sing and play music for the sake of singing and playing music. They're fantastic at it, and it helps to preserve traditional music - the kind you don't hear on the radio. But my favourite place to play informal music, simply sitting around in a pub jamming with friends, is on the Scottish Isle of Arran. Over the years, I met a lot of friends from the folk scene and camping on Arran, and a large group of them eventually moved there to settle down. So, whenever I went to Arran, I played with the whole gang - Geordie, the banjo player, Zoe, the great singer, Johnny, who played the tuba, concertina, and pennywhistle... and several others. We used to play in the local pub next to the village hall, and it was always a lot of fun.

Those Arran friends embraced the Rambling Man style wholeheartedly, but not all of my old friends saw the point. I used to go out for a beer with the guys from Partick who were either unemployed or worked in the shipyards. They'd make jokes about me after I'd left to perform. They recognized that I was unique... but I recognized that they were all the same. I had simply chosen to live differently and to appear differently. That can be perplexing for some people. There was no manual. The only difference between us was our definition of success. To those who didn't understand what we were up to, success meant getting a certain type of job or achieving a certain level of financial security, but to Rambling Men, your most coveted type of success is gained through the strength of your spirit and the richness of your world experience. It was about being yourself rather than what you thought you should be. Our heroes could range from folk singer-songwriter Hamish Imlach - who lived in a council house with a family but was one of us - to the famous folkies: Wizz Jones... Clive Palmer. They blew the bill at a club before sleeping on someone's floor.

Hank Williams, who sang "Long Gone Lonesome Blues," is my all-time country music hero and is buried in Birmingham, Alabama. He was The Boss. When I was a kid, his music meant a lot to me. His grave was surrounded by a stone border. You aren't supposed to take one, but I couldn't help myself. Hank spent the majority of his life in Birmingham, but he arrived in Nashville as a huge international star with eleven number-one hits. He died at the age of twenty-seven while doing drugs and drinking in the back of his car on his way to a gig. 'Let that serve as a lesson for you, m'boy.' That's what my father had to say about it.

I enjoy going to places where I can hear extraordinary, unusual live music, such as the band that performed at a high school football game in Texas. The band consisted of 350 people and twelve xylophones! I'd never seen a group of twelve xylophones before. They sounded like a brass band and were fantastic. And the choir had 300 people in it - for a football game! It was nothing like a football match back home: no pies, no Bovril, no chanting of taunts about a personal sexual act directed at the referee. A large, animated crowd attended. A woman was trying to get my attention, but I didn't get the game. My life story.

Bob Dylan at a concert hall in Canada was the best live music I ever heard while travelling. He didn't even bother to look at the audience. He played his piano against the side of the stage, never turning to face the audience. You never know what you'll get with him. He was a genius. The ultimate Rambler. Almost all of his songs are about being a Rambling Man, with lines like 'Where I'm bound, I can't tell' and 'I'm a-thinking and a-wonderin' walking down the road'. Yes, he was never one to stay put.

I used to earn money as a busker while hitchhiking around France before I could get proper gigs as a folk singer, so I know it takes a lot of guts to be a street performer. Your audience will always be utterly unpredictable. Since then, I've always enjoyed discovering great street musicians, especially when they're doing something I've never seen before. In Australia, I discovered some excellent buskers, such as India Bhauti, a one-man band I met in Sydney. It was a delight to see him performing strange electronic drum music while wearing a solar panel on his head that powered his homemade instruments. And Johannes O'rinda, who demonstrates extraordinary full-body coordination by whistling classical music while conducting with his arms. Then there was the sensational Kokatahi Band, who performed 'bush music' with accordion, fiddle, banjo, drums, spoons, and other instruments.

When I was driving up on my skidoo in an Inuit town, I witnessed something extraordinary. There was a girl singing in an unusual manner. She was facing another girl who had her mouth half-open and was making shapes with it, allowing the first girl to project her voice into the other girl's mouth and the echo to produce various noises. This was throat singing, and it was a very unusual sound. 'How are you doing that?' I asked as I approached on my bike. It's incredible!' Then the first girl's head turned around, and I realised she had a baby in the back of her anorak. 'I know! He's doing it!' I exclaimed. That style of music-making blew me away, and it's still a mystery to me. They made a rare and beautiful sound.

I'd like to tell you about the most amazing impromptu musical performance I've ever seen. It was a private one, with only me and one other person witnessing it, and it remains a high point in my life. Remember how I told you about the first time I visited Malta, after our plane was struck by lightning and we had to land there for repairs? My second trip to Malta came almost as unexpectedly. It was completely unplanned. My manager was going there for a couple of days to do some business at the time. Clients were filming on location in Malta for the film Popeye, starring Robin Williams. 'Would you like to come along for the ride?' he inquired. 'We'll laugh about it.' 'Sure.' I'd met Robin Williams before, on a TV show in

Canada. He'd teased me about my green leopard-print suit, which he dubbed my "Irish Tiger." My manager and I went to the Popeye set, and Robin came in and looked at me as if his memory was whirring, and then he said, 'Canada!' 'Yeah!' I exclaimed. When I first met him in Canada, he was well-known, but I had no idea who he was. 'How do you make a living?' I had inquired. 'I'm a performer.' He was charming. We hit it off right away.

We all got together on the first night I was in Malta: me, Robin, Ray Cooper, the percussionist, a genius banjo player named Doug Dillard, and Harry Nilsson, the brilliant composer and singer. I'd been a fan of his music for years. He was composing music for the film.

That night, the plan was for us all to get shitfaced. We started drinking and everything was fine until Harry said to me, 'Before you can become one of the gang - a Member of the Knights of the Maltese Cross - you have to write your name on that castle where everybody can see it!' He pointed to a massive, towering limestone fort that protruded from the landscape up a steep hill. Everyone looked at me as if thinking, 'Surely he's not going to fall for that? Undaunted, I scaled the hill and scaled the tower, writing BILLY in large white letters on it with chalky white stones I found lying around.

We ended up in a nightclub after completing our primary mission (getting shitfaced). That's where things got heated. The legendary roadie Booby Daniels had arrived, and he was chatting up a woman next to me, as is his wont. There was a Maltese guy on her other side and after a while, he mumbled something to Booby, and Booby mumbled something back, and then the Maltese guy hit him in the head with an ashtray. It was a true cowboy brawl, with people walking backwards and kicking. We all rushed out of the club Outside, Booby stumbled and knocked down the marquee after taking another one on the chin. Everyone then dispersed for the night. We dropped Booby off to get his injuries and likely concussion treated, and then it was just me and Harry. 'There's a guy here who plays great guitar,' Harry said. He works out of a garage. We ran into this guitarist on our way back to the hotel, but he hadn' brought his guitar with him. There was a piano sitting there, a terrible mess. It was green in colour. So Harry sat on a bar stool above the keys, fiddled with the instrument for a few moments, then turned to me and asked, 'What do you want to hear?' "Remember Christmas," I said. I really like that song of his. It was one of the best moments of my life when Harry played it just for me and the guy in the garage. There aren't many of them in a pound. Malta appeals to me. I enjoy its unique sites, such as the prehistoric G gantija or Gargantuan Temples in Gozo, which predate Egypt's pyramids and are the world's oldest freestanding structure. People back then were obviously enormous. Big doors, big steps - those people had to be massive. They could even have been large aliens. It's a lovely site, and you can touch things when you visit. They don't care because there aren't signs everywhere telling you to keep your hands to yourself. Ninu's Cave in Xaghra, Gozo, is my favourite cave in the world. It's a small cave discovered by a man named Joseph Rapa while digging a well beneath his house. He kept his discovery a secret for a long time because he was afraid the government would seize his home. It's now a small tourist attraction that people enjoy because it's uncommercial. You enter through the house's front door. When someone answers the door, you say, 'I'd like to see the cave, please.' 'Certainly. 'In this manner.' You make your way past family members who are simply going about their business in the house - cooking dinner, watching football on TV, and attending choir practice for the local church - which is the highlight of the entire visit. A door next to the bathroom leads to the wee cave. You descend some stairs to find yourself in front of some limestone formations known as 'The Elephant' and 'The Organ' by the family. You can try to see the resemblance for a few moments, but eventually a family member will tell you that your time is up. You drop a couple of euros into the box and are led out the door. There are no T-shirts, no gift shop, and no hard sell of trinkets. Brilliant.

I also visited Calypso's Cave in Gozo, which is said to be the location where Ulysses met and fell in love with the nymph Calypso during his travels. Ulysses, after all, was the first rock star, wasn't he? Going on tour and swishing around the world... with Penelope at home weaving her tapestry, and Calypso being the beautiful groupie he fell for and lived with for years, right? I'm in favour of it, but don't tell Pamela. My entire childhood was haunted by the Jesus statue, but I eventually discovered better art that didn't scare me - and I even came to appreciate some of the art that did. On Sundays, my sister Florence would take me to the Kelvingrove Art Gallery and

Museum, where I was introduced to geniuses such as Salvador Dal, Vincent van Gogh, Paul Gauguin, and Rembrandt, and by the time I was a folk singer, I was meeting some of the brilliant Scottish artists such as John Byrne and Sandy Goudie, both of whom became my friends.

I knew a lot of Rambling Men who enjoyed drawing. They carried a rolled-up sketchbook with them when they travelled. Some of these rambling artists were good, while others were not. Others I knew created items out of silver paper. My friend used to make horses out of the silver paper inside cigarette packets. He'd peel off the silver paper and draw a horse with his fingers. It took an extraordinary talent to create this miniature horse with the mane and tail flying upwards as if galloping. He'd hand it over to someone, and they'd ask, "Did you do that?" That's incredible.' I knew a lot of guys who did similar things, like making something out of string or performing small tricks like juggling glasses without spilling the water. It was a way for me to meet new people. That was never something I did. My specialty was being amusing. And I enjoy making music. But I did have a desire to draw myself... I just didn't think I could.

When I was in Los Angeles many years later, I met a guy. He was a filmmaker who wanted to collaborate with me on a film. I can't recall his name, but I didn't completely trust him. Not because he was untrustworthy, but because he was clueless about how to raise funds for that film. I was afraid I'd be wasting both his and my time. However, during one of our meetings with him, he asked, 'Do you draw?' 'I can't draw,' I said. 'You can, you know.' he said. He took out a pen. It was a pen that looked like a fountain pen but came to a point like a ballpoint pen. 'Look at something you want to draw and just draw it,' he said. Allow yourself plenty of time. If you make a mistake, try again. You'll be surprised at how much it pleases you.' That it did. I drew my Walkman, and it was very good. I was overjoyed that I'd drawn something I recognized.

That was all going through my mind when I sat down to draw for the first time while on tour in Canada. I used to go for walks in freezing weather, which is where my art began. I was bored and staying in a hotel in Montreal. I decided to go for a walk because the television offerings were particularly bad. In Canada, there is a type of rain that instantly turns to ice and sticks to you. It sticks to your coat, your neck, and your face, and it's painful. I waited as long as I could before ducking into a store. It was a pet supply store. I looked at the goldfish, budgies, dogs, cats, and snakes, and that was pretty much it. 'I'd better leave,' I reasoned. I went outside and walked a short distance until I came to an art shop directly opposite the hotel. I went in, and looked about, and then I found some coloured felt-tip pens and some sketchbooks and I thought, 'I'll draw. 'I'll mess around.'

I started drawing tropical islands, but they weren't realistic ones. There were red-and-white striped trees and other unusual sights. It was as if a slew of thoughts and information were just pouring out of me onto the page, and I liked it. That was my first step. I showed it to Pamela when I got home. 'I know it's bad, but do you think it'll get better?' I asked. 'Please tell me the truth.' 'It is,' she replied. It is improving.' So I persevered. Experimenting. I'm not sure why I did it. I had no intention of ever having art exhibitions or allowing others to see them. I considered showing them to my friends. Perhaps one day I'll be brave enough to say, 'Look at that... I drew this, what do you think?'

I continued to draw and found myself doing strange things. I used to draw stripes as the background, and the sky was also stripy, but then I changed my mind and began making the humans stripy and the sky something else. I'm not sure why I made those choices; they just seemed right at the time. I could go on and on. Then I began forwarding them to my management office. When my manager's wife became pregnant, I drew a pregnant woman with a visible baby inside, and she loved it. I kept sending drawings to the office, and everyone had favourites and was fighting over them. Then my manager took them to a gallery, and the people there wanted to be involved - though I had no idea what that meant at the time. What if that meant drawing a certain number of times per day, week, or month... I wouldn't want to do that. But if these people are foolish enough to hire me as an artist and believe in me, then fine... and here we are. I'm astounded by how other artists communicate with me. They're encouraging and say they like my work. They appear to appreciate the fact that I do it. They don't treat me like I'm a snobbish entertainer who sells drawings because he's famous, which I appreciate. Maybe some people think that, but they don't tell me...

I LIVE AT THE EDGE
OF THE UNIVERSE
LIKE EVERYBODY ELSE

Lovely. Auckland is a great city. Wellington gets all the 'capital' type of attention. But Auckland was the first city I landed in, and the first city in which I played, and it has a place in my heart. It has terrific art shops. I bought some nice pottery there.

I sat astride the large 'lost purse' sculpture in Melbourne, Australia. Angel by Deborah Halpern, commissioned to commemorate Australia's colonial bicentenary, and Melbourne sculptor Geoffrey Bartlett's Messenger in the National Gallery of Victoria are two examples of fantastic sculpture in Melbourne. Brilliant. Outside, there are sculptures that look like huge, colourful sections of pipe, with children sitting around them having picnics. I also like some of the supersized creations, such as Antony Gormley's Angel of the North, the largest sculpture in Britain that looks over Gateshead. I've come to believe that people should always be surrounded by sculpture and paintings, so I enjoy seeing large murals on the sides of buildings, such as those on Belfast's Shankill Road, which features fantastic, colourful loyalist art. In 2009, the Pontiac, Illinois, local government invited 160 artists to visit the town and paint murals on the walls of the town buildings on Main Street. They probably wanted to make it more cheerful. Some of the murals resemble Victorian advertisements, while others depict events and people from the town's history, and they truly bring the place to life.

It's fun when public art attracts controversy and irreverence, as has happened with the monument I saw in the centre of Dublin officially titled Anna Livia (The Spirit of the Liffey) but widely known by names like 'The Floozy in the Jacuzzi', 'The Whore in the Sewer' and 'The Biddy in the Bidet'. That's fantastic. In Cardiff, I saw some excellent sculptures made from road signs. Cardiff, Cardiff, Cardiff. All of this, plus Shirley Bassey...

Sydney does wonderful things. They set up sculpture walks' where you can walk down a path and see an open-air exhibition of works by Australian artists. There's one in the city centre, in the grassy areas of the Domain and Royal Botanic Garden, and another called Sculpture by the Sea that I've seen in Bondi. You walk two kilometres along a coastal path above the sparkling water and white sands of Bondi Beach and Tamarama on Sydney's North Shore, seeing various types of sculptural art set on sand, set into rocks, or planted in grass. It's breathtaking. That's a big advantage of having a consistent climate: you can rely on the weather to behave for something like that. If they

tried it in Scotland, the artists would be in tears. 'Oh my goodness!
'My little papier mâché piece has become soggy yet again!'

I met Preston Jackson, a brilliant artist who created fantastic solid-bronze castings of people in his community, in Chicago. He told me he irritated some people, and I replied, 'Yeah? Me too.' Preston's African American bronze people are stunning, with wonderfully amusing characters capturing aspects of Chicago's street life. Preston was both amusing and enlightening. We were both laughing about Pat Boone's rendition of Little Richard's hit "Tutti Frutti." Boone, who was white and Christian, had no idea the words had such strong sexual connotations - bible in one hand, unwittingly singing about sex. Preston also showed me the 'Green Book,' a disturbing travel guide for people of colour travelling outside their communities that was first published in 1936. It contained life-saving information about where they could sleep, eat, and find doctors, as well as lists of places they should avoid after the sun went down. What those people had to deal with - and in some cases still do - is mind-boggling. I had a conversation with Natalie Cole in Los Angeles a few years ago. She told me that her famous father, Nat King Cole, couldn't stay in the hotel where he was performing in the 1950s and couldn't even walk in the front door. He had to go through the kitchen.

During my travels in America, I came across a variety of oddities, including the Toilet Museum. However, I was underwhelmed. You've kind of seen twelve toilet seats, but the owner had five hundred all displayed on his walls. A toilet seat once saved my life. I was performing in an Australian town where Tiny Tim had performed the week before. They had some unusual visitors, and I was one of them. Iron Knob was a nearby town, and the crew and I went there on my day off. We were in Iron Knob's pub, and there was a swarm of loudmouth yobs gathered around the bar. It was the type of old Australian pub where men ruled. Some of those pubs even had a trough running around the bar where men could pee while finishing their next pint. I was wearing earrings, which drew some unwanted attention to myself. Behind the bar was some kind of trophy - it was a toilet seat with inscriptions and miniature trophies on it. When I got up to get a round for my crew, a big loudmouth behind the bar asked, 'Does she know you took her earrings this morning?' 'Who took your picture out of the frame?' I asked. That made him feel better. Everyone laughed. 'That's my boy!' he exclaimed, asking, 'What are you having?' And he won the game. It's great when a great line comes to you at the right time. Especially when it prevents a smack in the mouth.

I went to the Cadillac Ranch near Amarillo, Texas. Stanley Marsh 3 was an eccentric millionaire who created some iconic graffiti-covered pieces of art that represent the American love of automobiles in the 1970s. I saw large Cadillac slices lined up in the desert, pitched at the same angle as the Great Pyramid of Giza. The artist encouraged people to repaint the slices with new graffiti, so he cleans everything off every now and then to create a new canvas. I'd never done any graffiti before, but I went for it. Some of the pieces already had my name written on them. 'Hello' was written in black spray paint.

After leaving the Cadillac Ranch, I became aware of the Californian desert all around me. It's the kind of place hippies used to 'turn on, tune in, and drop out' in the 1960s and 1970s. I used to hear about it in the 1960s and was envious of that kind of life. I saw another interesting permanent exhibition at Elmer's Bottle Tree Ranch - sculptures made of collected bottles and other items such as guns, toilet seats, hubcaps, old fans, and rocking horses - hanging from trees and displayed in unusual ways. It was insanely imaginative work.

I once visited a barbed wire museum and couldn't decide whether it was art or not. I had no idea there were so many different types of barbed wire, each with its own set of knots and designs, and each with its own name. Joseph Glidden, for example, invented "The Devil's Rope." Before barbed wire, there was free-range grazing all over the state, but people began fencing off their land, especially if it had water. This resulted in numerous fights and even deaths. Some types of barbed-wire splices - those jagged bits that cut your trousers - fascinated me. I'd always wondered why they cut at a right angle. There was even a display of World War One barbed wire in the museum. The British trench wire had more gaps than the Americans. They were obviously a gentler race of people...

I visited a wonderful artists' community in Darwin, Australia, which was populated by weavers, designers, and painters. I was obsessed with their art, particularly the bright designs painted on cars and corrugated iron. The location was essentially a cooperative endeavour, with all food caught or gathered being brought back to share. I was blown away. They have a lot to teach us. In recent years, there appears to have been an explosion of First Nations art. I met Jimmy Pike, a well-known Walmatjarri artist whose work can be found in all of Australia's major museums and art galleries, as well as in several international galleries. As a child, he lived in the Great Sandy Desert before becoming a stockman. After getting into trouble, he went to Fremantle Prison and learned to paint with unconventional materials. It was an honour to meet him and observe him paint.

Several Australian artists have had a significant impact on me. Ken Done is a genius. And he's very approachable. He'll talk about his art all day. He doesn't hide or say, 'I don't get it,' like I do. I flew across Sydney Harbour in a seaplane to film an interview with him. We landed in the water next to his beach house, and Ken picked me up in a small rowing boat with his dog, Spot.

Ken uses intense blues to paint Sydney Harbour or morning glories. He taught me that it's more important to paint the feeling of, say, walking by the harbour at night when it's still hot and the sky is warm than it is to depict something realistically. He assisted me in seeing things clearly and using my eyes. To recognize when a storm is approaching. Storms are common in Sydney. Pink lightning strikes. I get out of bed now to watch. Ken had seen my show the night before we spoke. 'I envy the instant feedback you get,' he said. If I do something worthwhile, hopefully the dog will bark...'

Ken taught me how to make art while I was hanging out with him. 'I'd love to be able to draw as well as a five-year-old,' he said. That newness. People often say, "I can't draw." People should draw and paint, in my opinion. It's just that they have a presumption that it will be true. It should only be the sensation of a cow, a flower, or a person.' I wasn't drawing much at the time, but I was getting started. 'I've done some drawings,' I told him. Should I send them to you?' And he replied, 'Sure.' However, I didn't do it. It has something to do with your art being yours and being a part of what you're doing. I learned from him that I should love my own work and not question it or myself about what it is. It is the self. It is not required to provide you with answers. Ken taught me that I don't need to explain it because it just... is, and that brings me joy. Ken was extremely helpful in teaching me this. He gave me confidence.

Asher Bilu, a Melbourne artist, is also very talented. I paid him and his wife Luba a visit, as well as their garden bird Billy Blackbird. I used to hear the bird ask where I was after I left. I frequently feel very close to people who have dedicated their lives to the arts. Brett Whiteley, for example, was not only brilliant but also a joy to be around. He personified everything fun and Australian. I first met him in Sydney at the Townhouse Hotel's rooftop swimming pool. I was introduced by Mark Knopfler. 'Brett's an outstanding artist,' said Mark. But I wasn't sure what he did at the time. That is said about a lot of people. But Brett was full of life, ideas, and running and jumping around. I knew I liked him at first, but I wasn't sure what to make of him. He was dressed casually, with a strange little hat perched on his wild curly blond hair. He reminded me of Harpo Marx. He was a truly lovely man with a brilliant mind. He adored and frequently quoted all of the books he had read. I sent him a copy of A Confederacy of Dunces, my favourite book. He began dropping by the Townhouse to see me. He'd just walk in, and they'd call up and say, 'Brett's here,' and he'd take me out for Japanese food. He was a big fan of sushi. Had a strong desire to live. Spontaneous. When Pamela and I invited him to our rented house in Pearl Beach, he jumped off the verandah into the swimming pool. That was dangerous. He used to go to the zoo just to see the famous Tasmanian devil, a vicious meat-eating marsupial. Because the creature would never come out of his lair, Brett would throw coins at him to entice him to snarl. Brett liked the colour of his mouth because it was red.

Brett had a great laugh and could make me laugh out loud. He came to my show and then bet me a hundred dollars that I couldn't do a completely different show the next night without repeating a single story or comment. I finished it! Twice in two and a half hours! But when he threatened to return for a third night, I had no choice but to tell him to fuck off.

Brett presented me with a plate depicting a small bird. He imagined himself as a bird. Little birds have flown in and made a big impression on me twice in my life. The first was a jackdaw that landed on my head as a boy in Rothesay and said, 'Hello!' I was on the verge of dying. The second bird was named Brett Whiteley, but he died at the age of fifty-three. He was a charming, funny, and outgoing man who enriched my life beyond measure.

Some art is simply beyond my comprehension. I once attended the University of Northumbria's arts and design degree show, which featured a number of compelling installations, drawings, and paintings. I can't say I understood what was going on, but I enjoyed it. I was presenting a TV show in which we featured the art show, but I didn't know what to say about it. I never want anyone to think I'm closed-minded when it comes to art - or anything else. I'd hate for someone to say, 'Billy dislikes irregularity,' because then someone else is bound to say, 'All-Bran for him!'

CHAPTER 9
HOW TO BUILD AN IGLOO

'If you don't like the weather, hang on for twenty minutes,' they say in Scotland. When the sun comes out, they declare, 'We'll pay for this!' I love how dramatic the weather in Scotland can be. You can practise standing at 45 degrees with that kind of wind. In the Highlands, you can hang-glide if you put on a raincoat. Leave in a cape and arrive in Oslo. In any case, that's where all the trees are. Where do the dogs pee? piss in the air while lying on their backs? People in Bergen are exclaiming, 'Fuck! 'The rain stinks of piss.' If you go on vacation there, don't bring a beach ball. You'll give it to a kid, and it'll end up in Denmark. People go shopping with their weans strung on bits of string.

I'm assuming you're familiar with Scottish history in New Zealand. Hamish Dreich and Donald Dreary led a large boatload of Presbyterians to the country. They all had those little disapproving mouths that look like an arsehole with a slice of lemon slipped into it. They landed in northern New Zealand, and the sun was shining, and all the Moris ran out to greet them... and you know how that goes. 'Uggghhh! Take a look at those people who have their tongues out! We know what that means: filthy buggers! People who have tattoos...! 'We need to go south, south, south!' They arrive at the top of the South Island. The location was fantastic: beautiful sun shining down, mountains and palm trees... life is fucking great! 'Nope!' They continue south to Dunedin, saying, 'Horizontal drizzle - excellent! Let's come to an end here! Calm down. We can complain here for centuries!'

I don't normally care about the weather, but as a rambling entertainer, you have to in certain places. If you live in Calgary or Alberta, you'll hear a radio announcement in the morning telling you how much time you can spend outside with your face exposed. It could be five minutes, twenty minutes, or whatever the temperature and weather conditions require. After that, you must go inside. As a result, you must pay attention and follow instructions. Extreme weather is only a nuisance in places with milder climates. For example, if you live somewhere where it rains a lot, you get tired of being wet and, while there's no real harm in it, your clothes are constantly soaked. You must wear waterproof clothing and carry an umbrella, and the weather can even affect your health. And, if you're touring as an entertainer, as I was, you don't want to catch some strange virus that's going around.

First and foremost, do not let your wife pack your bags. She'll put things in that she thinks you should take. You'll end up with four jackets when only one or two are required. You'll need one casual - perhaps a denim one - and one heavy waterproof. Take nothing you don't need. Pack wisely. Place items inside your shoes. And only bring one bag. A Rambling Man never carries more than one bag.

Get off the street when it's too hot. Get a fan to help you cool off. It's a pain, heat. There is nothing you can do about it. Wear no man-made materials as underwear. Wear cotton clothing. Wearing nylon or any of its relatives will make you feel terrible. It'll give you the impression that you have a bunch of bananas down there. Your feet will also stink. But not from underwear, but from socks; wear only cotton or wool socks. Change your socks before getting off a long-haul flight. You'll be surprised at how much better you'll feel afterward.

When I stepped off the plane in Coober Pedy, Australia, I thought I had stepped into the aircraft's exhaust. But then I realised it was the hot wind. It's not warm; it's boiling hot. I'd never been anywhere so scorching. I got on the motorcycle and rode across the airport, but even in the slipstream, I couldn't cool down. It was hell for me to have to ride around a lot while filming in Coober Pedy. But I never stopped wearing my leathers.

When riding your bike, you should always keep the weather in mind. Layers are required in cool climates to ward off the worst of the weather. Even if the weather is fine, you should still wear your leathers in case you slip. Leather protects your tattoos as you scream across the gravelly road. Wear something smooth, like a shiny shirt, under your leathers so that if you fall off, your skin slides under the leather and you don't get scraped. Wearing gloves is also a good idea. As I previously stated, meeting the road is unavoidable, so it is best to be prepared for it.

The worst weather I've ever experienced while touring was about thirty years ago in Canada, when there was a three-week whiteout. I had had enough of it. Canadians are used to dealing with extreme weather, but I was sick of the blizzards. I recall being in Toronto around midnight and being driven down a street in the financial district. I'd done a show, and we'd stayed at the venue for a while at the end. I was returning to the hotel. When we came to a stop at the lights, an enormous gust of wind came off the lake, hit the back of the car, and shoved us forward about six feet. It was amazing to feel the weather mess with you like that. It was grave. You can't go outside in that weather; it's not pleasant.

I don't mind being cold at all. It comes naturally to me. But there has to be a reason for it. Travelling in the Yukon was fantastic; it lived up to my expectations. Some of the old miners' architecture can still be found. Because the buildings are built on frozen matter, they frequently lean to one side and have begun to fall over with the passage of time and global warming. The pubs still have a hillbilly vibe to them. In one, the locals put you to the test by giving you a drink with a floating thumb in it and telling you that you must let it touch your lips to be considered a real guy; it's part of some local legend. Some of those male-dominated traditions irritate me. Men's toilets, where men pee in a trough - isn't that fucking primitive? Women each get a door and a small room, while men get a trough. Men occasionally approach me while I'm peeing.

'Do you look like Billy Connolly?'

'Yeah...' 'Oh, hello!' Give out.

'Fuck it!'

The coldest I've ever experienced was in the Arctic. I flew from London to the Canadian Northwest Territories in 48 hours, landing at the world's most northern airport. Then I took a skidoo up north. I had a fantastic trailer for my skidoo that I loaded with my rucksack, roll mat, cooking equipment, sleeping bag, groundsheet, and extra clothes. I had a saw to cut the ice, an axe, a knife, and the same Lee and Enfield rifle I'd used in the Paras. And, of course, my banjo, which I used to perform 'Campbell's Farewell'. But I didn't sing it. All that nonsense about Bonnie Prince Charlie would have been inappropriate for the occasion:

The prince who should have been our king wore the royal red and green.

A more attractive young man has never been seen than our brave royal Charlie.

I drove to a town of 135 Inuit people, my trusty trailer piled high with my necessities. They were fantastic. They built me an igloo, and

I watched closely because I was told that I would have to build one myself later on. The next day, after venturing even further north, I set up camp beside an ancient iceberg. This was the point at which I would have to try to build my own igloo. Making your own shelter is a very basic thing to do. Every time I saw a house I wanted to buy, I'd be standing in its grounds with a desperate need to pee. It happened again beside that iceberg when I was deciding where to build my igloo. I was desperate to pee, so I must have chosen the right location. It must be a primal need to mark one's territory.

I worked hard to build my own igloo, but I made a critical error early on. You must carefully construct the ice bricks, laying them at precisely the right angle to ensure the walls' strength. Because it's all about the angles, if you make a mistake early on, you're doomed. The snow bricks are slanted and must be precisely placed so that it all goes up like a cone to a narrow bit at the top and then closes. That's what I've been taught. That's all well and good, but it's not easy when you're freezing and have to dig all that bloody snow out of the ground. The man who built it for me had been doing it his entire life. He was around seventy years old when he built the Taj Mahal of igloos right in front of my eyes. It was a work of art.

Inside, igloos are beautiful. When you enter your little tunnel, there is no wind. You can hear the wind outside and feel incredibly clever. You turn on your lamps and lay down your groundsheets, and the room begins to sweat and seal itself up. It's fantastic. A very pleasant way to live. But when I tried to build an igloo, it collapsed on me about a third of the way up, so I gave up. I recall sitting on it and talking to the camera. By accident, I called it a pyramid.

I wished I had done better, but I was pleased to have completed one-third of an igloo. I ended up sleeping in an ice tent. To pitch a tent in such an environment, you must first dig a hole with a spike. Then you dig another hole nearby to create a small tunnel large enough to fit your finger through. The guy rope can then be attached and tied to the ice. Lovely. It was a fantastic tent. Unfortunately, I began to have recurring nightmares about the ice cracking and me falling through in my sleeping bag and drowning. That was stupid of me, because six-foot-thick ice doesn't crack enough to fall through. But, once I calmed down, I found the tent to be cosy. My tent had a musk-ox skin on the floor and a comfortable sleeping bag; in fact, I was so comfortable in there that I didn't want to leave. I wanted to stay home and practise my banjo. I slept on yak-skin groundsheets and dressed in sealskin clothes that stink to high heaven, but nothing bothered me. My water supply was the size of an iceberg, pale blue in colour and made up of frozen fresh water. It was the most opulent water tank I'd ever seen. I was overjoyed. And nobody in the entire world was north of me.

When I went on excursions, I rode in sleds pulled by dogs. The dogs adore their keepers, but they are completely out of control. They aren't pets. They are wild and hardy creatures who sleep in the snow. People throw them frozen meat - whale and seal - which they must lick to soften before eating. They fart like there's no tomorrow when they eat that kind of food. You're out on the virgin snow, just you and the dogs swishing along, and it's fantastic - except for the clouds of fart floating back at you. The sky turns blue. And when they spit, it sticks to their bums' hair, so when they fart, the shit comes flying off towards you. You're just enjoying the fresh air when this overwhelming wave of dread washes over you.

Overall, it's entertaining. It's fantastic to be the guy in the Arctic. I ate commando cuisine. SAS supplies are no longer the jawbreaker biscuits that military food once was. It's fantastic. It arrives in an envelope, frozen. It's delicious after you add water and heat it up. There are fantastic stews and desserts like apple pie and custard. Classy. That's right up my alley. I was also given a nice little cooker. I wore sealskinz socks with caribou-fur socks. I simply inserted my bare feet into them as instructed, and my toes were as warm as toast. Okay, I probably wouldn't have been welcomed outside Harrods in my politically incorrect attire, but I didn't care.

I enjoyed being alone for extended periods of time. The Arctic has a silence that you won't find anywhere else on the planet. You can hear the silence. You are aware of it. 'God, it's quiet, isn't it?' you say to people. As if the silence had simply made a noise. It has heft and presence.

It was sunny most of the day for a while, and then the snow came, and it snowed for about three days. It was great fun to ski around in the fresh snow. It never rains in that area. It's raining little twinkly rain. You know how when you magnify a snowflake, it has those little legs and a geometric shape? Millions of tiny ones descend and land on you. You're just waiting for the music to begin, 'tinkle tinkle tink'. I thought it should be called fairy dust because my girls would love it. I always left messages for my girls when I was on the road. I would cut out pictures from magazines or books, paste them onto a sheet of paper with little tidbits about wherever I was, and fax them home. But there was no way to communicate in the Arctic. I was completely cut off from the outside world, which I grew to appreciate as the days passed.

I grew tired of the camera crew coming around during the day, filming my every move. I wished I could spend more time alone. I became very attached to the virgin snow that surrounded my tent. The crew arrived on skidoos and trampled the entire area. I knew I had no right to be that selfish and mean, but I couldn't stop myself. They'd throw cigarettes at me in the snow, and I'd say, 'Look at the state of this place!' 'It's not good enough!' I began to grumble. 'You must treat it with dignity. 'This is where I live!' I was being completely honest. It got to me because the film crew would all leave around five o'clock in the afternoon, leaving me alone in the Arctic.

When I say 'alone,' I mean an SAS soldier - Paddy from the Irish Guards - who was camped out at sea, watching for polar bears. He had stated that if they were coming towards me, they would be coming from that direction. I never saw any, but he used to tease me about it. He'd get on my two-way radio and sing the 'Teddy Bears' Picnic', 'De doo de doo de diddly doo'. It was a lot of fun. But I had to be prepared for polar bears if they got past him. There's only one way to tell if a polar bear is nearby: if it growls. That is unlikely to happen. You're done if it likes you. I kept my gun ready to fire. I was told that if the bear is far away, you can scare it away by firing over its head. 'What does "far away" mean to a polar bear?' I inquired. 'More than 300 yards,' he says. 'But what if it doesn't?' I wondered. 'If it's still coming at you, kill it for your own protection.'

To be honest, I believe Arctic conditions provide the ultimate challenge for a Rambling Man. On the one hand, it's the ideal environment for someone who wants to wander alone and be self-sufficient, but on the other, you're reminded that there's no salvation if you get into serious trouble because there's no bugger anywhere nearby to lend a helping hand. There were also psychological challenges, which most Rambling Men do not face. Outside my tent, for example, there was an iceberg. It was considered small, but it stood about twenty feet tall and fifteen feet wide. And that was just the visible portion. Fresh water floating in seawater forms icebergs.

The seawater rises and falls with the tide, shoving the iceberg up and down, rubbing against the sides of the hole it's in and making a polar bear-like noise. Grrrrrrr Oooooh. I'd hear this while inside my tent and think, 'Oh fuck!' I'd get out of my sleeping bag, take out my rifle, and put on my jacket. I'd go outside and find nothing. Then I'd take another look because I'd heard that polar bears know their noses are black and cover them with their paws. That's wonderful, but I had to be extra cautious. Because it was always daytime when I was there, I just went to bed when I got tired. After eight hours, I'd get up and check my traps before wandering around looking for footprints. I was reminded of Grizzly Adams. I saw fox, seal, and bird prints. The aurora borealis would appear in the evening. I'd stand in the snow with this incredible exhibition just for myself.

I developed a siege mentality, saving bits of string and other materials. I'd tell them to go back to their hotel and leave me alone. I wasn't scared; in fact, I was ecstatic. I'd get up, play some T. Rex on my banjo, go for a couple of hundred yards on my scooter, then come back and make myself some porridge. I don't have a care in the world - and a little T. Rex to cheer me up. I made my own daily video diaries. 'You're sitting at home, eating your fish supper by your electric fires,' I said to the camera during one of them. You're dressed casually in your slippers... and you're wondering, "Where does he go to the bathroom?""Well, I'm not going to tell you." In fact, I dug a hole in a nearby neighbourhood and had to bare my arse there. It is not simple. You must be quick. That was one of my main concerns before embarking on my journey. 'In severely low temperatures, it's best to do it in the tent and use the heat,' according to the SAS survival handbook. 'Not this soldier,' I thought. I'll just be a little colder and risk getting frostbite on my bum if I go somewhere else.'

It reminded me of the wilds of northern Scotland, where the environment is always larger than you. It forces you to be humble, as if nature is saying, 'Watch your step, sonny boy. You'll be in big trouble if you step out of line here.' There wasn't a single living thing to be found. Normally, you'd see a small seagull or something, but not this time. There is nothing. Every night, the iceberg creaked and croaked. They have been around for millions of years. Straight from the glacier, and extremely slick. But after a while, the iceberg's noises didn't bother me as much. They kept me entertained. According to David, my Inuit teacher, there were people in them. His forefathers were encased in ice. There was a sense of presence there. You can feel the silence due to its extraordinary density. There was another iceberg nearby that resembled Jesus - a man with a beard wearing a crown of thorns - but I was the only one who could see it. Perhaps I was losing it... I couldn't care less if I was. In any case, I was certain that having a Rambling Man sensibility was the best way to survive such a test.

The Inuit were charming people who seemed perfectly at ease in that harsh environment. They had nice customs and ways. If they have a baby, they do not name him or her until they know who he or she is. Until they realise who has returned among them. They'll notice a trait in the baby of a deceased person and decide it's that person. So it's perfectly acceptable for a boy to have a girl's name. The names are for everyone. Having your mother's name is a lovely thought. And Akiatuk, my guide, told us that he had been given his mother's father's name, so if she didn't behave, he would. He'd tell her, 'Daughter, behave.' And when they hunt and catch a seal, they do not get to eat it; it is for the benefit of the entire community. And they'll get some when others go hunting.

I moved to the other side of the bay, about six hours away, near the end of my time in the Arctic. I sailed across the sea and arrived at Craig Harbour, but there was no harbour and no Craig. It's just ice. A post office had bear-claw marks where a furry creature had tried to get in through the window. A massive, hairy, ravenous beast. Despite this, I felt like I was in the most peaceful place on the planet that night in my tent. And I discovered I had ringing in my ears. I hadn't washed in five days and didn't want to wash anymore. On the fifth night, there was a blizzard, so I had to pee in a polythene bag. Because it was frozen in the morning, I went out and buried it with pomp and circumstance.

Later that day, I discovered some polar bear prints near a bloody seal carcass that had been ripped apart and scoffed. Foxes and ravens had also had their turn. It was very depressing. I noticed a lovely seal looking at us before nervously dipping into its hole. Aside from that, I saw no wildlife. However, because the creatures are all white, they are difficult to see. There could have been millions of them in the area, but I'd never known. I set out to try to reach an ice floe, but it quickly became very cold. A blank page. I had no idea where I was. It was terrifying and dangerous. It was a valuable lesson in my smallness. I was just a city guy stranded in a lonely place. Despite my rambling tendencies, going to the Arctic taught me that Rambling Men are drawn to places where community thrives in some way. It doesn't have to be densely populated; it could just be a small group of people, but being alone in the wilderness would be difficult. I returned to my base, knowing I was leaving the next day, relieved that I hadn't been eaten by anything... but there was still a whole night to go.

In the Arctic, I learned a lot. I adored the solitude, the ruthless wildness. And I discovered that I could be content on my own with just my thoughts for a while. I'm not nearly as terrified of myself and my imagination as I once was. And I'm no longer afraid of extreme weather because I've experienced it all - high, low, wet, dry, and everything in between. I have, however, witnessed some wind-related devastation. Three hundred miles northwest of Chicago I was riding my trike when I got caught in a rainstorm near the start of tornado country. The county of St. Louis has more than its fair share of these natural weapons of mass destruction - about 300 per year and there were five just before I arrived. I drove into the ruins of a township that had been completely destroyed by a tornado 166 miles long and 1.5 miles wide. The entire town had been destroyed in thirty seconds. A survivor said he knew it was coming the moment his ears popped. He described the sound as "like a freight train." A family was searching the rubble for valuables. One woman had discovered her engagement ring. Her wedding gown had also survived, albeit mud-splattered and with a small hole in the seam. But those people were exceptional. They had lost everything, but their spirits were high. They were already remodelling their homes to include an extra bedroom and a larger porch. That's the spirit of a pioneer. Perhaps we should stop whining about the weather. Count our blessings more often. It may seem churlish to say, 'Things could be worse,' but tornadoes and waterspouts have been known to lift alligators into the air. Consider one of those large bitey reptiles landing, alive and well right next to you and your pancaked house.

I've never experienced a hurricane. In fact, I'm secretly troubled by the fact that Pamela and I now live in a place where winds can whoosh you off without so much as a 'please' or 'thank you' and dump you in the Cuban jungles. We had a major hurricane shortly after we moved here. Pamela pushed me onto a plane to California as soon as she heard it was coming, but I've told her I want to stay for the next one. The authorities order everyone to leave, but the locals continue to party.

I once attended a hurricane party, but the hurricane never arrived. It happened while I was on tour with Elton John. We had been performing at Madison Square Garden. Backstage, word came that there was a hurricane warning for Long Island and that someone was throwing a hurricane party. We all piled into buses and cars and drove off to join in the fun... but the guest of honour never showed up. Being in a posse of celebrity storm chasers, on the other hand, was a lot of fun. We were, to be honest, unprepared for a hurricane, but that didn't bother us; drugs and alcohol were probably involved... Yeah, drugs and alcohol were always involved.

CHAPTER 10
THE LAST RESORT

SOME OF THE COOLEST PEOPLE I KNOW ARE
DECOMPOSING RIGHT NOW.

Graveyards have always appealed to me. I enjoy reading the
gravestones. Many of them bear the line 'Forever Young' by Bob
Dylan. Pish. We are not eternally young. We're always decomposing.
'Forever Dead' would be a better title. 'Asleep' contains a lot of
nonsense. No, I don't believe so. I believe he is dead. Some are both
funny and savage. 'Stick your nose here and I'll set about you'. I was
thinking 'Jesus Christ, is that the time already?' on mine, but Pamela
was unsure, so we settled on 'You're standing on my balls!' in tiny
wee writing.

Glasgow has some lovely cemeteries. A fan once confronted me in
the street, saying, 'Eh, Big Yin? You're exactly like us...!' 'What
exactly do you mean?' 'Didn't you drink wine in the cemetery?' That
was an outright lie. I've never drunk wine in a cemetery before. But,
okay, I've shagged over there...

Egypt has my favourite graveyard in the world. It's the City of the
Dead, an ancient site. It's a remarkable place, about four miles long,
with houses for all the dead people. They number in the thousands.
It's exactly like a huge, eerie housing estate. Years ago, I performed
in Cairo for a Scottish man who asked if I could entertain Scottish
workers restoring a famous old grand hotel. He provided a
knowledgeable tour guide to show me around. I thought she did an
excellent job translating many of the inscriptions on the tombs. We
mostly hear about pyramids in Egypt, and if you were a real head
honcho in ancient times, you got the full gold pyramid with all your
stuff inside. However, in later centuries, wealthy individuals found
their final resting place at the City of the Dead. Bereaved families
used to stay in the mausoleums for the customary forty days of
mourning and would return to the deceased person for memorials and
vacations, but the buildings essentially remained empty - until
recently, when living people began squatting in them. There are now
many thousands of breathing 'tomb-dwellers' living there. That is
Cairo's response to poverty and a housing shortage.

Glasgow's Necropolis is another sight to behold. Many old Glasgow worthies, including the nineteenth-century author William Miller, who wrote 'Wee Willie Winkie,' are buried in the Victorian cemetery. 'The Laureate of the Nursery,' his gravestone reads. The Necropolis was the final resting place for wealthy people. The tombs, headstones, and monuments were all very expensive to install. These people had larger houses when they died than the majority of Glasgow residents had when they were alive. There are wealthy merchants and many people who helped build and maintain Glasgow, the empire's second city. Charles Tennant is buried there; his main business was a chemical works in St Rollox for coal processing. To me, it sounds like rhyming slang. Some Lords Provost are buried in the Necropolis, as are shipbuilders, artists, publishers, and engineers, as well as World War II war graves. There are also some beautiful tombstones and monuments. It depicts how Glasgow used to be.

I've never been afraid of cemeteries. In fact, I was always made to feel welcome there. When I was a kid, I used to wander around graveyards for no apparent reason. It was just lovely there. I wanted to walk there by myself and be at peace. It was a difficult period in my life. I couldn't get along with my professors. I couldn't get along with my father and his two sisters, Mona and Margaret, at home. They were all at a loss for words when it came to me. They considered me to be a complete waste of space. I once volunteered to attend a bishop's funeral, which was to be held at Glasgow Cathedral. I knew him because he was a priest at a parish close to my school. There were priests of all ranks present, from the lowest to the highest. I travelled with two other guys. But my jacket had a hole in it, and the teacher in charge of us said, 'Connolly! 'What are you doing wearing that jacket?' 'It's the only jacket I have,' I explained. 'You were warned about this before you volunteered, that your uniform had to be in very good shape,' he explained. And he drove me home. It was all thanks to my Aunt Mona. She never repaired anything. If something had a tear in it, she would enlarge it. She once set fire to my school tie. I wasn't present at the time, but I discovered the remains. She was a victim.

In the United States, I created a television series about death called The Big Send Off. It felt good to talk about death and tell the truth. You can only avoid it or lie about it for so long. You can't fool yourself any longer after learning about the Buddhist way, the Mexican way, the Islamic way, and all these different ways of dying and being buried. You must consider death from a practical standpoint. That gives me a great sense of relief - a sense of release. Nobody expected anything from me when I made the series - just my thoughts - so I was able to be completely honest about it. I investigated the one certainty in life: that we will die. You see, news of my death has been greatly exaggerated. A few years ago, I received hearing aids on Monday, heartburn pills on Tuesday, and news that I had prostate cancer and Parkinson's disease on Wednesday. Despite this, I was never in danger of dying.

Death and how we deal with it fascinates me. We avoid discussing death, but it is a 21-billion-dollar industry in the United States. I went to a pet cemetery where a guinea pig burial cost $550 for the plot, $350 for the coffin, and $1000 for the marble headstone. Then I went to a funeral directors' convention in Texas, where they were promoting embalming fluid party packs, shampoo for dry, lifeless hair, and blankets with life-size pictures of the deceased - you can sit with it for a drink or sleep with it. There were zombie-proof steel coffins on display, as well as hot-rod hearses and the option to reserve rockets to the moon for your ashes. The eco death-suit was threaded with mushroom spores; the fungi feed on your decomposing body and return you to the Earth as human compost. You're useless to any Earthling, so it disposes of your body in an orderly manner without bothering anyone. I'm not sure what I think about a mushroom eating me. There is a theory that mushrooms originate in space. They arrived on meteors and remained. I'm convinced. They reproduce differently than any other species on the planet. And they have the appearance of aliens, not humans. Octopuses, too.

There are numerous options for how you can be buried these days. The Neptune Society scatters ashes beneath the Golden Gate Bridge, with no relatives present because that is how the deceased person desired it. I went along and found it deeply moving, with the ashes trailing in the water and a trail of flowers trailing behind the boat. That's something I'd like for myself. Eric Idle, one of my friends, has expressed interest in having fireworks and dressing up. Maybe even a cash machine in his cask to make it a worthwhile visit. His song 'Always Look on the Bright Side of Life' has long been a favourite for funerals.

Some say you die the last time your name is called. The Mexican Day of the Dead commemorates those who have died. Some people choose to get memorial tattoos. One woman got a peacock tattoo for her grandmother because she always had a swarm of peacocks on her property. It wasn't until she got the tattoo that she discovered her grandmother despised peacocks and used to shoot them.

I've met people who believe science is the answer to death and can provide eternal life. A large group of scientists believe that ageing is a disease that can be treated. In Buddhism, when you see a dead thing on the road, you say to yourself, 'That is the Way of all things, and it will be the Way of me too.' That appeals to me. I met a guy who claimed to believe in everything because 'that way I can't be wrong!' He was sick and on the verge of death at the time. For a dollar, he let me try out his coffin. It looked like a box of clothes from a high-end store. It was made of cardboard and was ready to burn. He was buried in a skeleton suit, as he had requested. They removed the skeleton suit from him before he was cremated and sent it to me. Pamela and I were living on the tenth floor of a Fifth Avenue apartment in New York when this THING arrived. It was a fantastic skeleton suit made of rubber with zips, but I don't dress up for Halloween, so I had no idea what to do with it. I didn't want it in my life, so I had to figure out how to get rid of it. Our apartment building had a trash chute that you could use to send your trash down to the bins on the ground floor, so I decided to throw the suit in there. It was sent to hell.

As for me, I haven't decided where I'll be buried, but instead of a headstone, I'm thinking a table on an island in Loch Lomond for fishermen to picnic on would be nice. During The Big Send Off, I especially enjoyed visiting the 'green' graveyard, Eloise Woods, a nine-acre plot of land in Texas. Ellen Macdonald, a neuroscientist, was the first to open it. It was a simple idea - you could be buried in a natural way. Someone would dig a hole for you, drop you in it, and invite your friends to say 'Cheerio'. You can be buried with your pet if you want... though he might not like it if he's not dead. It's endearing. Excellent condition. Everything about it is excellent. One man was buried beneath his chair. They simply sat him in his chair and covered him in dirt. Every year, five million gallons of embalming fluid are poured into the ground, which is bad for the environment, so this is the solution - a green burial ground. Families can dig their own graves and mark them with simple markers such as flat stones. It seemed like a refreshing change from our culture's denial of death, where people are made up to appear alive and simply sleeping.

I also liked the Columbarium in San Francisco, which is a massive structure that serves as a repository for human ashes. There are memorial walls where people can leave items that the deceased person liked, displayed as dioramas - little plastic soldiers, flowers - things that meant something to both of them - on a small shelf. There were many snow globes, including some from Hawaii to commemorate a memorable vacation. And photos of Scottish men in kilts who died far from home. When left to their own devices, people do wonderful things. Some people are so imaginative and playful, even in the face of death. The most creative headstone I've ever seen was a hat and a beer keg. While he was still alive, he had his own corrugated iron coffin made. While he was alive, he used it as a wine rack in his living room, and then he was buried in it.

Making that documentary altered my life. I used to think about death and my life and ask myself, 'How will I be held responsible for it when I come to judgement before God?' I no longer believe that, though the whole thing remains a mystery to me. Meeting the people I spoke with during the series was very reassuring. They were all lovely; I didn't meet a single unpleasant person. The Compton, Los Angeles, drive-through funeral parlour was a blast. Visitors could sign the visitors' book outside before driving through to pay their respects. In the window was a coffin with a dead woman inside. They raised the coffin so you could see her better. The parlour's owner was Peggy Scott Adams. 'Death is a part of life,' she said. She was fantastic. She made her customers feel good. She'd worked as a backup singer in a soul band. We had a little dance when we got to the chapel and sang, 'Goin' to the chapel and we're gonna get ma-aa-arried...'

Hillside Memorial Park is Los Angeles' most prestigious Jewish cemetery, with residents including the Max Factor family and Al Jolson. It's a bit like the theatre - being interred at eye level commands a premium, while the cheapest seats are up high, 'in the gods'. And you don't have to be stuck with it if your circumstances change; cemetery brokers can assist you in cashing out if necessary. Families will sometimes disinter a body, have the remains cremated and then sell the plot. I discovered that there are even theatrical agents for the dead. On one headstone, there was a lovely inscription: 'In memory of Sophie Kravitz. My wife and I met at a travel agency. She needed a vacation and I was her last option.'

In contrast, just outside of Los Angeles, a lovely Muslim holy man named Gulad guided me through the process of burying Muslims. He talked about death being simple. The family has authority over the washing of their loved one's body in Islam. Death is viewed as a leveller. A simple van transports people to the cemetery. If people are unable to pay, the mosque will. Gulad was one of the most pleasant people I'd ever met. He was the head of a mosque, and he was so kind to the dead and to me. 'We wash our own people,' he said. Then we take them to the cemetery in a van.' He and I were both laughing about the van. 'I think I'm a van guy,' I said. 'Oh, I'm definitely a van guy,' he said. In his traditional manner of death, loved ones accompany the deceased person into the grave and point them to Mecca. They surround them with earth and then cover them with it. Gulad spoke of it with joy and understanding. He left an indelible impression on me. He took me to the mosque and demonstrated how to kneel. The carpet has been specially designed to indicate where your knees should be.

'Do you believe in God?' he asked.

'I don't know,' I replied. I've struggled my entire life, wondering, "Does he believe in me?"

He threw back his head and roared. 'Can I use that?' he asked. I replied, 'Yeah.'

We clicked like a house on fire. It was fantastic. Everything changes after we die. If a relative dies, he is taken away in a box, and we are not allowed to see him until he is returned in a fancy polished box, wearing make-up. In comparison, our burial customs appear ridiculous.

My daughter Amy was with me as I prepared The Big Send-Off. Because she had studied Mortuary and Forensic Science, she was the researcher. She was full of stories. They told her to keep an eye out for 'jumpers' at the gravesites. People apparently frequently jump into graves and are injured as a result. They should break their legs. Amy was taught how to recognize, stop, and catch them. The emotions that wash over you at funerals are strange. I found myself crying as the father of a friend was lowered into the grave. I'd never seen his father before - I was just carried away by everyone else's emotions. Then I remembered a line from a Gerard Manley Hopkins poem we read in school, 'Spring and Fall,' and realised it had to do with my own mortality: It is Margaret you mourn for.

But, no matter how beautiful your funeral is, you never know what will happen in the future. John Knox, Scotland's Reformation leader, insisted on being buried within twenty feet of St Giles' Cathedral. It was a reasonable idea at the time because there was a graveyard adjacent to the kirk. However, the area was eventually paved over and is now a parking lot. As a result, Knox's grave is commemorated by a small plaque in parking space number 23. It just goes to show: who knows if all those people who pay a fortune for burial plots will actually end up there? If the price is right, council members can play all sorts of little tricks. Zoning? False alarm.

I didn't leave my heart in San Francisco while filming that TV show; I left another part of myself in New Orleans. I was experiencing severe stomach pains, and they discovered that two pieces of metal from a previous operation had become adrift. They had to force their way through my willy. I'm sure you just winced. Isn't that fate worse than death?

The best death scene I've ever seen was in a pub on Glasgow's Byres Road. I was drinking a pint and waiting for my uncle to arrive. He didn't, so I ordered a pint and went on my way. But then a guy came in, looking a little flustered, and did that Glasgow thing I love: he blurted something out in the middle of our conversation. 'It's fucking murder!' he exclaimed. We were all sitting around, puzzled, looking at each other. 'I cannae go in...' he continued. I'm not sure why I went in the first place!' 'What's that?' I asked. 'I'm at a wake upstairs,' he explained. He was in the top flat of a tenement above the pub, it turned out. 'I don't even know those people,' he said. My wife is familiar with them.' 'They're being nice to me, but I don't know them,' he explained. It's a strange atmosphere. I'm sorry I came.' He must have sensed my attempt at being sympathetic because he turned to me and said: 'I have to go back up. 'Do you think you'd come up with me?' 'I don't know them either...' I said. He stated, 'That doesnae matter.' 'We're friends,' he said. We'd only recently met, but that didn't seem to be a problem. 'We'll get a half bottle of whisky...' he said. And so we did, and we went upstairs. This is a well-known custom in Scotland. You go to the house where the deceased lived and sit in the hallway with cups of tea and coffee, talking happily about them. Then the official part begins: someone invites you to an inner room where the coffin is to bid farewell. You'll be given a drink and invited to join in on the official toasts. You wish them well, and people comment on how much they liked them: 'He was a good man. 'A man of integrity.' And a funeral was always a good excuse for the local alcoholics to fill up their jars. They'd simply join the queue. Nobody enjoyed chasing them away. They'd put on a black tie and pose as a friend of the deceased. It was always the same guys, everyone knew.

So there we were, sitting around drinking whisky and making funny faces at each other. We tried to strike up a conversation, but they were a rather stuffy bunch - and I never found out how the man's wife knew the deceased person. But then the door opened, and an unusual-looking head emerged. This head had a massive Adam's apple, massive cheekbones, a huge bulbous nose, and pointed brows. He appeared to be in great distress. 'Hello!' he said. 'My name is the corpse's brother.' Those were his exact words - one of the most amusing and strange lines I've ever heard. 'Hello! I'm the corpse's younger brother. 'Do you want to come in and drink his health?' So I had no choice but to enter. In any case, there was a nice atmosphere and whisky to drink his health - to see him off. The deceased man was lying in an open coffin, and I couldn't help but notice how similar he looked to his brother.

I've always been fascinated by death rituals. Something wonderful has occurred in the Clyde. Govan Road in Govan, where the shipyards were located, runs exactly parallel to the Clyde River. And when someone in the shipyard died - someone well-known and liked, such as a shop steward, foreman, or manager - there would be a procession down the road. People would line the street and remove their caps as they passed in a wave, similar to the Rockettes dancers in New York, but with bonnets. Seeing the wave of caps being doffed all along the street was lovely. It was a thoughtful gesture. I discovered that when funerals are held in American hobo communities, there is a similar outpouring of respect. Everyone wears a burlap strip and taps the gravestones with their walking sticks. The hobo euphemism for 'died' is 'caught the Westbound'.

I enjoy funerals as well. My manager used to be perplexed. He'd say things like, 'Billy - Even if you haven't seen someone in 25 years and they die in another country, you'll hop on a plane to see them.' That is correct. I just enjoy seeing people leave. It's significant to me. Boys from the school. Clydeside apprentices. Welders. It's similar to a high school reunion. Seeing all the people from that time and place - that world I once lived in. I gave a speech at Jimmy Reed's funeral. It was beautiful. I just told him some amusing stories. Regarding his singing style. 'I'm passing strangers now...' Crooning. And everyone was laughing because they remembered him. However, I am not the only one who enjoys funerals. People in Ghana love funerals so much that there is a demand for a four-day week so people can recover from their hangovers. And what's not to love about some Taiwanese funerals, where the family hires 'electric flower cars' - trucks with mobile stripper stages?

We all know you have to be careful how you talk about the dead. When my friend Stan's wife died, I wrote to him, "She always used to sneak up to my end of the dinner table to have a good laugh." I always remember her doing that... laughing.' 'Yes, Billy, I remember it well,' Stan replied. She frequently expressed her boredom...'

The contents of this book may not be copied, reproduced or transmitted without the express written permission of the author or publisher. Under no circumstances will the publisher or author be responsible or liable for any damages, compensation or monetary loss arising from the information contained in this book, whether directly or indirectly. .

Disclaimer Notice:

Although the author and publisher have made every effort to ensure the accuracy and completeness of the content, they do not, however, make any representations or warranties as to the accuracy, completeness, or reliability of the content. , suitability or availability of the information, products, services or related graphics contained in the book for any purpose. Readers are solely responsible for their use of the information contained in this book

Every effort has been made to make this book possible. If any omission or error has occurred unintentionally, the author and publisher will be happy to acknowledge it in upcoming versions.

Copyright © 2023

All rights reserved

Printed in Great Britain
by Amazon

54750401R00069